THE JOY OF HEX

MODERN SPELLS WITHOUT ALL THE BULLSH*T

NINA KAHN

CASTLE POINT BOOKS

NEW YORK

CONTENTS

THE JOY OF HEX

INTRODUCTION

HELLO WITCHES, B*TCHES, ASPIRING WITCHES, ASPIRING B*TCHES — however you identify at this point in your spiritual journey, greetings! I'm happy you're here. I hope you're ready to embrace your mystical inner empress and dive into the empowering world of spells and rituals.

If you're reading this, then I'm guessing you probably have at least a passing interest in witchcraft. And clearly, the universe agrees that it's time for you to start developing (or strengthening) your relationship with the mystical energy that is all around us, all the time—and the mystical energy that is *within you* at all times, too!

There's an undeniable mystique to the craft of performing spells and rituals. If you've ever explored the limited but influential canon of witchy teen movie offerings, in which cool and mysterious high schoolers dressed in all black fill their bedrooms with ritual candles, buy herbs at witchy shops, put love spells on their crushes, and play games like "light as a feather, stiff as a board" with supernatural results, then you *know* what I'm sayin'. Witchcraft has an allure. But casting spells isn't just about being a witchy, crystal-wielding, candle-carving, tarot card-reading baddie. (I mean, it's a little bit of that, but I digress.) It's also about stepping into your own power, connecting with the undeniable power of nature and the earth, and owning what's *yours*—as a woman (or whatever you identify as!), a witch, and as a bad lil' b*tch, too.

WITCH RULE #1: YOU ARE F*CKING POWERFUL

The world we live in is a wild one. Between social injustices, global pandemics, a sh*tty job market, *way* too many selfie filters than our mental health can safely handle, and the earth casually getting a little bit hotter every day, it's safe to say that modern times are freaky, weird, and kind of out of control. Navigating these nutso realities while also trying to manifest love, self-confidence, money, success, ride-or-die friendships, spiritual enlightenment, *and* personal growth is no easy task.

But what if I tell you that you have more power to make sh*t happen than you think? What if you could use the resources you *do* have (even if they're limited!) in a more effective way? I'm not just talking about pouring blood, sweat, and tears into something and hoping you have enough privilege to carry you to your destination. What if you found that you had an unlimited resource *inside of you* that wasn't tied to money, status, looks, follower counts, or anything else?

Well, you do. Let's talk about **energy**. We're obviously *surrounded* by different powerful energies all the time, but we're also filled with energy ourselves. We are conduits for it. Energy allows us to get dressed in the morning, call a friend, form opinions, and do all the other things that we do throughout our day. We have energy, and we constantly make conscious choices about how we're going to use it.

We also have a more mysterious type of energy within us—an energy that's making choices *for* us. This energy is what makes our hearts beat, heals our skin when we get a cut, and ensures we keep breathing. By connecting with the mysterious energy *within* you using witchcraft-based spells and rituals, you can start using it to your advantage—and affecting the energy all around you, too.

Witchcraft isn't a magic pill. I am not saying you can overcome every bummer life circumstance with the "power of positivity" or anything like that. Honestly, sometimes sh*tty things happen to good people, and you can't just *MaNiFeSt* and *GoOd ViBeZ OnLy* your way out of it. But it's good to know that amid all the chaos, all the craziness, and all the uncertainty, you have a little bit of power within you that no one can take away, no matter *what* circumstances you face. And while you can learn to enhance your power using crystals, candles, and cards (as we'll discuss throughout this book), at the end of the day, those are just cool bonus tools. The real power at the heart of witchcraft, and at the core of the spells and rituals you're about to learn, lies within *you.*

HERE'S WHAT THE SPELLS AND RITUALS IN THIS BOOK WILL HELP YOU WITH:

- Creating magick using simple, accessible tools (and stuff you already have at home).
- Accessing and following your intuition and divine energy source.
- Trusting yourself, girl!
- Making your day-to-day life more mystical.
- Focusing your energy toward things you actually *want* in your life.
- Evolving into the most authentic, badass version of yourself.
- Using magick as a tool to reach realistic goals.
- Connecting to earth's natural cycles like the goddess you are.
- Having fun. Duh!

HERE'S WHAT THIS BOOK IS NOT GOING TO HELP YOU WITH:

- Waking up with a suddenly perfect life (if someone says they have a spell for this, be wary, sister).
- Complicated spells made with countless obscure ingredients (no eye of newt or toe of frog required here—promise).
- Focusing your energy on negativity or harming others. (Nope. Get your bad vibes the f*ck out of here!)

- Practicing witchcraft blindly or doing rituals that don't make any sense (because understanding and connecting to the spells and rituals you perform matters).

- Promoting snobbishness and pretentiousness that makes people feel left out because they aren't witchy, powerful, or knowledgeable enough. Witchcraft is for everyone who wants to explore it; spells can work for *anyone*, not just ordained high priestesses.

WITCH RULE #2: F*CK THE RULES

No human being gets to control or dictate the personal and intimate relationship you form with your higher self and with the divine nature of the universe. If you find a spiritual path that resonates, that's awesome. If you don't, that's okay, too. Just keep learning, experimenting, and of course, being intentional—and by being intentional, I mean putting thought, purpose, and confidence into your magickal acts. (Even if you don't feel confident yet, you'll get there!)

This book is a journey into the witchy world of modern-day spells. While "witch life" can be filtered and glittered up and put into a very aesthetic package, spells and rituals are more than just trendy. They're ancient tools for changing your life, harnessing your personal power, and connecting with the world around you in a deep and powerful way. And you're about to learn how to work 'em and make them your own. Get ready to step into a whole new side of yourself—and step out into the world as a brand new witch.

CHAPTER 1

THE WITCHY BASICS

GETTING TO KNOW THE WONDERFUL WORLD OF WITCHCRAFT

You're no basic b*tch, but everyone's gotta start somewhere!
Getting clear on the ABCs and 123s of witchcraft will give
you a solid foundation for your future as a full-fledged,
spell-casting, ritual-practicing witch.

WHAT IS WITCHCRAFT?

The word "witchcraft" is used to describe so many different practices across so many different cultures that it can be hard to define—but it usually describes practices that involve *magic*, such as performing spells, divination (a.k.a. communicating with spirits and higher powers), and other metaphysical arts. Generally, the spiritual beliefs associated with witchcraft center around nature and the earth's natural cycles, which is why modern-day pagan-based religions, like Wicca, are often associated with witchcraft in the mainstream. But witchcraft is and has been practiced by people of all different religions (or no religions at all) around the world. No matter what your belief system is, you can practice it too, connecting with it by casting spells and performing rituals.

Call your spell practice witchcraft, b*tchcraft, spellcraft, arts and crafts— whatever the f*ck you want, darling. But whatever you call it, know that it's also a journey into the core of yourself, into your relationship with your own energy and the energy of the world around you.

OK, SO YOU'RE A SELF-PROCLAIMED B★TCH . . . BUT ARE YOU A SELF-PROCLAIMED WITCH?

We all know you're a bad b*tch. But how do you feel about being a *witch*? Let's dive into some terminology here.

I'm going to use the word "witch" pretty regularly throughout this book, but you don't have to identify as a witch in order to conduct spells and tap into your personal power. Anyone can do it—it's just a matter of being willing to focus your time, energy, and intention on your personal spiritual practice.

For some people, claiming "witch" can be empowering. Live it and love it, witch sister. But I know that, to others, the word can feel a little intense and come with some heavy and not-always-positive connotations. Of course, the same could be said of the word "b*tch" (although I hope it's obvious that when I say it, it's in the most loving and empowering way possible!). Many women have taken back that word from misogynists (who've used it to degrade people throughout history) and turned it into a term of endearment. All of which leads me back to *witch*: Isn't it interesting (and kind of bonkers) that some people might literally feel more comfortable being called a "b*tch" than a "witch"?

Why do witches get such a bad rap? Despite all the social media witch-fluencers filling up our feeds with tarot card pulls, curated shots of their altars, and poetic captions about manifesting goddess energy, "witch" can still, for some, conjure up creepy visions of old women with black pointy hats and wart-covered noses flying on broomsticks and putting curses on innocent muggles as they cackle sinisterly over boiling cauldrons full of hair and bones. Um, not cute. Kinda scary. And *definitely* not the aesthetic we're going for. This is real life, y'all, not the Halloween aisle of a discount superstore.

In addition to being deeply un-cute, this wicked-witch-of-the-west stereotype is also *not* a trustworthy representation of a modern-day witch or her modern-day craft. They're just a dusty ol' caricature. A witch can look like anyone, believe in anything, and use any tools they'd like. In fact, a witch can look just like you! Because being a witch is about a lot more than collecting jars full of unidentifiable but allegedly magical herbs, filling mystical bottles with bubbling potions, and dancing naked under the moonlight with your coven. It *can* include all of those things (you do you, girl), but it doesn't *have* to look like any of that.

EMBRACING THE DIVINE FEMININE IN YOU

By common definition, a witch is simply "a woman who is believed to have magic powers." With such an enchanting meaning, why would anyone twist it into something negative? Well, it puts "woman" and "power" in the same sentence.

Powerful women (and the powers *possessed* by women) have long been downplayed and devalued. But times are changing. And no matter how many times society might try to bury the power of the ~divine feminine~ (aka the goddess-y feminine magic that's inherent in all humans), it can't be snuffed out. This mystical inner power is here to stay—and it's completely unlimited in its potential.

Enter witchcraft—which is just one of many ways you can connect with and channel this personal power (and it happens to be a particularly fun and exciting one). The use of ritual magick and energy work that's been practiced by women (and people *all over* the gender spectrum) for thousands of years, has *always* included the work of finding power within yourself—of healing, of taking charge, and of connecting with the divine feminine energy that's inside of every living thing on earth.

And despite how it sounds, divine feminine energy isn't about sex or gender. In nature, there's an inherent balance in everything—light and dark, hot and cold, and also masculine and feminine. These elements work together in symbiosis to create the perfection and magick of the natural world. The divine feminine and divine masculine are two halves of a whole: the divine masculine is strong, creative, highly active, structured, and fire-like; the divine feminine is gentle, intuitive, receptive, free-flowing, and water-like. Both are equally important and powerful, and everything contains a balance of both. The divine feminine really gets a chance to sparkle in earth-based spiritual practices like witchcraft, because our lush, life-giving planet is the epitome of divine femme vibes. This mystical energy is ever-adaptable, open, and powerful in its beauty. And we all have access to it.

But sadly, instead of embracing the fabulous divine feminine that's in all of us, some people are threatened by it. So much so that some women and other marginalized groups who are able to find power, value, and worth in themselves are considered . . . dangerous. Just look at what happened during the Salem witch trials in the seventeenth century; if someone even *suspected* a woman of being a "witch" (which they directly associated with Satan and evil), she could be publicly hanged.

When society doesn't honor the masculine and feminine energies of our nature, it's even more important to get in touch with your divine feminine power (by practicing spells and rituals) and become the most powerful b*tch (and witch) you can be.

CASTING SPELLS AND F*CKING THE SYSTEM

That all said, using your personal power and divine feminine energy to connect with the mystical forces around you and bring forth changes in your life is more than just fun. **It's a full-blown statement against any person, idea, or system that has tried to trick you into believing the myth that you aren't powerful.** Because, b*tch, you are!

One of the beautiful things about the energy of witchcraft is that its power and strength comes from its beauty and gentleness. Conducting spells and rituals is a way to manipulate energy and create change using nothing more than your intention, intuition, and trust in the universe. The divine feminine is flexible, adaptive, and intuitive—there's no violence or brute force involved. In that sense, it's sort of a big "f*ck you" to the money-obsessed oppressiveness, physical violence, and toxic masculinity dominating modern-day society.

And the more you get in touch with your higher self and learn to work with energy, the more you'll realize that your worth does *not* align with the worth that society places on you. The size of your waist doesn't define your power. Your sexual desirability doesn't define your power. The jobs you (do or don't) get, the college you (do or don't) go to, and the amount of followers you have on social media do not define your power, either. At the end of the day your power lies within you—it is undefinable, immutable, nonnegotiable, and hella magickal—and it'll never leave you. It's built into your soul, sister. The sooner you realize how true this is, the more powerful you'll become.

Using witchcraft-inspired spells is a powerful tool for growth, discovery, and connection with the world around us—both the visible world of tangible things *and* the invisible world of energy. And your practice can look however the hell you want it to. There's no one single "right" way to do things—plus, labels suck anyway. Claim "witch" if you'd like, and claim it proudly, if you become comfortable with the term and feel it represents the spiritual work you're doing, but certainly don't feel pressured to do so. You can get to know your mystical energy and become a spell-casting queen using any title your heart desires. You call the shots!

ARE YOU A GOOD WITCH OR A BAD WITCH?

Like all forces of energy, spells and rituals can be used to help or harm, to do good or to do evil. Now, everything exists on a spectrum of course, but it can be helpful to stick to a moral code of sorts when diving into the world of spells, just to keep you grounded and guided.

There are some spells that are known to be harmful, such as curses. Curses are a naughty type of magick that are intended to bring bad luck to someone, or to otherwise f*ck them over or cause harm. The word "hex" is often used to refer to a curse, too—but it can also refer to a regular ol' spell. The title of this book is *The Joy of Hex*, but don't get it twisted. We're good witches (albeit bad b*tches), so we're not *actually* going to be putting curses on anyone. Okay?

Although there's no one religion that owns witchcraft, the one that's most widely associated with it is Wicca, which is a nature-based faith grounded in pagan traditions. Wiccans abide by something called the "Wiccan rede," which is sort of their witchy code of ethics, and it reads: *An' ye harm none, do what ye will.* **In other words, do whatever the f*ck you want in your personal practice, so long as you're not f*cking with anyone else.**

Do as thou wilt, you witchy baby, you. But if you're asking my humble advice, abide by the rede and stay away from the practice of fighting bad vibes with even more bad vibes (*especially* if you're new to witchcraft).

This means do not try to work spells that meddle in the free will of others (like putting a love spell on your crush) or that intend to harm someone (like cursing someone). That just leaves us with a whole lot of bad vibes and not much good. And if we're talking energy work, it's not great karma, either. So, should you do a spell to facilitate the cutting of ties with toxic friends? Absolutely. But should you do a spell to ruin the life of said toxic friends? Absolutely not.

SPELLS & RITUALS ARE FOR EVERYONE

You don't have to identify as a witch in order to conduct spells and practice rituals that tap into your personal power. Anyone can do it; it's just a matter of being willing to focus your time, energy, and intention on your personal spiritual practice. In fact, rituals and symbolic acts are present in all different religions.

You also don't have to up and get initiated into a coven or disown any of your current spiritual beliefs in order to work these spells and rituals—they're powerful and effective regardless of religion. Whether you're a Satan worshipper or a Catholic school valedictorian, I'm not here to judge. Working with energy through spells and rituals is an excellent way to 1) refine and focus on the things you actually *want* in your life, and 2) ground yourself and connect with the energy that's all around you (instead of ignoring it and letting all that potential magick go to waste).

Spells and rituals are open for business to anyone who wants to use 'em. You can combine your spiritual beliefs with witchcraft if you'd like. (In fact, I recommend it for maximum connection and vibey-ness!) But you can also perform spells as a separate practice, too. It's okay to hold unique religious beliefs *and* harness energy to shape your own reality. There's no rule that governs your ability to do both separately, or to combine them in your own unique, one-of-a-kind witchy practice.

MAGIC VERSUS MAGICK

You've probably seen the word "magic" written with a "k" at the end. Not your standard everyday spelling, but I promise its significance goes deeper than just trying to witch-ify the word for funsies. The word "magick" was put into use by spiritual practitioners who wanted to differentiate between the everyday usage of the word "magic" (which implies an illusion-based performance for entertainment) and the type of ritual, energetic magic that witches and other energy workers perform. Hence, "magick" was born; it refers to spiritual magic versus the sleight-of-hand, bunny-from-a-hat type of magic. Because honey, *your* magick is no trick—it's real and powerful.

HOW DO SPELLS WORK?
THE RIPPLE EFFECT

Let's do an analogy here. Think of reality (the ether, the universe, the energy around us, *whatever*) as a large body of water. Compared to us, the body of water may be like the ocean, huge, massive, and full of waves that are controlled by the moon above. But all *we* have in order to create change on the surface of the body of water is a pile of pebbles. Doesn't sound like much compared to the energy of the great moon, does it? When we toss those pebbles into the ocean, we may not hear the splash, and it may not make waves—**but if you look closely, you'll see the ripple effect of those pebbles.** Out from the point where our pebbles hit the water's surface shoot rings of silent, circular, pulsing vibrations, stretching into the expanse of the ocean. We see that ripple with our own eyes. Other people see it, too. It's tangible, visible, forceful. It may not make a wave, but sometimes you don't need a whole wave. A ripple is enough to make magick happen.

When you put an intention into the universe, it causes a ripple effect in your reality. And those ripples make a *difference*. They shift the energy of reality in their own small way. They can change things. Does this mean that if a tsunami rips through your corner of the sea that your ripple won't be rendered effectively useless? Of course not! There are plenty of outside circumstances, beyond our control, that can shift the course of our lives and the situations we must face, regardless of a spell. (Like I said earlier, spells aren't a magic pill.) We can't make impossible things happen, but that doesn't mean that all your other ripples aren't still having an effect, large or small.

By taking what you want and distilling it into a spell, then communicating it via ritual to the universe using the common language of symbols, you're essentially giving the cosmic chef your order with immense clarity and gratitude—and that will likely bump it up to the top of the queue.

CHAPTER 2

A GOURMET GUIDE TO SPELL CASTING

EVERYTHING YOU NEED TO KNOW TO START SLAYING SPELLS AND ROCKING RITUALS

Knowing the basic tenets of witchcraft is good, but spells and rituals are the true heart and soul of this book—so understanding a little more about the mystical puzzle pieces that come together to create the magick of a witchy spell is vital.

SPELLS VERSUS RITUALS: WHAT'S THE DIFFERENCE?

Let's talk terminology. The terms "spells" and "rituals" are often used interchangeably—and quite frankly, you'll probably get a lot of different answers about the nuanced differences between spells and rituals depending on which witch you ask. However, spells and rituals *are* slightly different; and in the name of being a well-informed witch, it's important to understand what generally defines each and differentiates it from the other.

A **ritual** is an action or a series of actions carried forth with a spiritual purpose, usually (but not necessarily) involving the use of symbolic tools. A **spell**, on the other hand, refers more to your *intention*, and is typically performed with the hopes of producing a specific result.

These babies work in tandem. So when you take your intention (the spell), pair it with symbolic actions (the ritual), and empower it with your own energy, it all alchemizes to create powerful magick. **You can have a ritual without a spell (for example, to create or honor something). But if you perform a ritual with the intent to *change* something or achieve a desired outcome, it becomes a spell.**

I believe some of the most powerful magick takes place when you combine these two elements into a single act, as most of the spells in this book do. Let's break things down into more detail:

RITUALS. Rituals are about energy and performance. As mentioned, rituals are typically defined as a series of actions done for a spiritual purpose. During a ritual, you use symbolic and literal actions and tools to drum up energy, within and without you. When ritualistic acts are used as part of a spell (i.e., if you're stating an intention with words that express a desired outcome regarding future events or experiences), you use that energy to create a desired outcome in regards to a specific situation or aspect of yourself.

A ritual can (and often does) include a spell, but it doesn't have to. A ritual can also be carried forth to merely honor or connect with a particular energy, celebrate something, or create a magickal tool. Some examples include rituals to celebrate a full moon or a change of season; or rituals to honor a particular goddess or deity whose energy is meaningful to you.

SPELLS. Spells are about your intentions. Some people view spells as rituals that involve a desired outcome or shift at the end; spells direct energy toward a specific goal and intention. Because a spell is performed with a particular desired outcome, it almost always includes a verbal or written component, through which the intention is stated in words. Intention is a major driving force behind the creation of a spell. There is often (although not always) a ritualistic element to a spell, too.

A spell can be formed from any sort of desire. Some examples include a spell to help you heal from a gnarly heartbreak, a spell to inspire creativity, or a spell to protect you from the sh*tstorm of Mercury retrograde.

Just as spelling has us placing *letters* in a specified order to form a *word*, witchcraft's version of a spell has us placing *words* in a specified order to form an *intention*. Words are spells, and one of the defining factors of a spell is the *translation of our desires into words*. Spells are intrinsically linked to words and intention.

On the other hand, the word "ritual" implies a prescribed order of actions, which is common for both witchcraft rituals and everyday rituals. Think of the way people talk about their "morning rituals" or their "bedtime rituals"—these are really just routines; a series of actions that are repeated on a regular basis. When it comes to a spiritual practice, many witches perform rituals on a cyclical and repetitive basis, like moon rituals to connect to the energy of the lunar cycle, or rituals to celebrate the witchy holidays and to connect with the sun and Earth's energy.

THE MAKINGS OF A SPELL

Let's boil things down and simplify. There's a formula that you can follow when understanding the power of spells, and it consists of two main components:

✦ ENERGY + INTENTION ✦

Who brings these components to the table during a spell? Well, *you* do.

ENERGY IS EVERYTHING, so let's start with that. Energy is the potential to cause change. And of course, change is what we want—it's the goal of a spell. That's *exactly* why we want to collect a bunch of energy when we do spells, and why it's one of the essential ingredients of an effective spell.

The first law of thermodynamics states that "energy can neither be created, nor destroyed." I don't know much (ahem, *anything*) about thermodynamics, but this law simply means that energy is just *here*, all around us, buzzing and moving and constantly shifting forms. Crazy, isn't it? Think of the way energy comes and goes in different parts of your life. If we feel our physical bodies losing energy, for example, we can sleep, eat food, or even exercise in order to generate more of it again. This, in turn, fuels the energy of our thoughts, which can also affect the energy *outside* of our own minds. This is the ripple effect of energy in action. That's the pebble that creates a ripple on the surface of your life's ocean. Energy is here for our use. Nobody owns it. And it's constantly changing forms and switching hands.

Energy might seem elusive—sometimes we have lots of it, sometimes we can't seem to find enough of it. But don't be intimidated. Once you start getting comfortable performing spells, you'll find that you can often round up and take control of energy pretty easily by using some tried-and-true tricks.

So how can we bring on the energy? Of the many different ways to raise or collect energy for use in a spell or ritual, the easiest way is to use symbolic objects and/or perform some symbolic actions (a.k.a. rituals!). Symbols are a language, and they are an important part of spell work.

There are also lots of magickal tools that can be used to literally and symbolically bring energy into a spell. We'll get deeper into the tools of the witchy trade in Chapter 3, as these tools and mystical objects can be lots of fun—but you don't *have* to have a bunch of special tools to generate energy for ritual work or spells. You can generate energy yourself, using nothing but the power of your mind and body! This could be done through physical movement (think dancing your ass off to your favorite song), through sound (chanting or singing loudly, or clapping your hands), or even through the power of thought (like by meditating and visualizing something). And of course, we can't forget the ever-so-powerful act of simply writing and speaking meaningful words, which leads us to intentions.

Let's get intentional. Before you begin a spell, you'll want to know your intention. Having an **intention** to change or achieve something turns a regular ol' ritual into a spell. Witches normally express their intention in words. This might take the form of a chant, a mantra, or a statement

---

MY ALCHEMICAL ROMANCE

Alchemy is a concept used often in esoteric, occult practices, and it describes the seemingly magical processes of change and transformation—or, to simplify, of turning one thing into another. Like rubbing two sticks together and suddenly: fire. Like setting fire to wood and suddenly: ash. This almost-mystical transformational process is helpful to think about when doing spells, because in a spell, alchemy is what we want! We may not be spinning thread into gold or turning water into wine, but our goal is generally to turn one thing (our intention) into another thing (our reality). Incorporating physical embodiments of alchemy into our spells (using elements like fire, smoke, waters and oils, and more) can help remind us of the alchemical magick that we create through spellwork in order to turn our dreams and desires into tangible, real-world outcomes.

---

that's used to make your intention crystal clear. Why use words? Well, words have a *lot* of power. Think of the way we can affect someone else's feelings using words, or get what we want using words (ask and you shall receive, right?). Words are symbols that represent our thoughts, feelings, and desires. Words can also be commands.

With words, we're able to speak the invisible into reality. Our feelings, our desires, our hopes, and our dreams can all be spoken and made real and requested (and subsequently, even *granted*) using words. Thus, using our words in a ritual serves a double purpose: It can be the energy *and* the intention.

Intentions grow within our thoughts. When we use our energy to speak those actions aloud or write them down with words, that alone can serve as a ritual. There's power in speaking the words so that our ears can hear them; writing the words so that our eyes can see them; forming the intention into words in the first place, giving them a tangible form, changing them from an invisible, nebulous, formless thought into something perceptible to the senses. Speaking your mind is always a good idea—even when creating a personal and private spiritual practice for yourself!

BUILDING UP YOUR INTUITION

Knowing your intention requires good **intuition**. Some of us are indecisive or simply aren't used to being our own guide. That's okay! If that's where you're at, you'll want to build up your intuition—that inner voice that always tells you the truth and that "third eye" that notices things your conscious mind may not, which *always* has your highest good in mind, no matter what. Calling on and strengthening your intuition is a must when it comes to being a witch. You've gotta trust yourself, sister.

WAYS TO BUILD UP YOUR INTUITION

We live in a society that undervalues intuition, so it's easy to get into the habit of ignoring it, constantly favoring pragmatism over our gut feelings. But your intuition is really important, especially when it comes to doing spells and rituals. Here are a few ways to start developing your natural, built-in inner clairvoyant.

- **Make "intuition lists."** Try strengthening your intuition by taking the time each evening to write about things that happened that day and what your gut feeling told you about the situation. It could be an intuitive feeling about a person you met for the first time, a place you visited, or a conversation you had. You can also jot down any symbols that felt meaningful to you or that you felt represented a deeper concept. It may feel strained to try to analyze your experiences through this lens at first, but it'll become more natural the more you do it—and you'll probably find that your intuitive feelings get stronger, too.

- **Keep a dream journal.** Dreams are the playground for your subconscious mind, as sleep is a time when your rational brain gets a chance to rest and the rest of your brain goes wild. That said, getting in touch with your dreams (and paying attention to the symbols and messages within them) is a good way to clear out the cobwebs from your intuitive sense. It'll get you accustomed to the habit of retaining information that your subconscious offers to you, instead of immediately dismissing it before it has a chance to impart its wisdom.

- **Work with divination tools.** Divinatory arts, like tarot cards, rune stones, crystal pendulum dowsing, and flame gazing have been used by mystics throughout history to help them gain access to their inner wisdom—and these tools (which we'll discuss more in Chapter 3) can all serve as a conduit through which *your* intuition sends you messages, too. By working within these systems, you'll have a medium that allows you to explore your intuitive sense with a little more structure and tangibility. For example, instead of using pure intuition to get a read on a situation in your life, you can draw a simple tarot spread and allow the cards to serve as a liaison to bring your intuitive sense into your conscious mind.

HERE'S AN EASY RITUAL THAT WILL HELP YOU LOOSEN UP AND LEARN TO LET YOUR INTUITION GUIDE YOU.

MIND'S EYE INTUITION-STRENGTHENING RITUAL

◯ ◗ ◗ ◗ ◗ ◗ ● ◖ ◖ ◖◖ ◖◯

SOME MYSTICS BELIEVE THAT WE ALL HAVE A THIRD (INVISIBLE) EYE, a mind's eye, that we can use to get in touch with our psychic senses. If you're ready to activate your **third eye** and open a direct line from your intuition to your conscious mind (yes, please), this spell can get you comfy and ready to receive. You may even use it as an opener to another spell, if you'd like to clear your mind beforehand to allow for a clearer connection to your truth and desires.

GET IT TOGETHER

1 clear quartz crystal

Frankincense oil

---

1 Lay down in a comfortable and quiet place where you are free of distractions. Grab your clear quartz (which enhances and amplifies energy, and gives clarity) and anoint it with some frankincense oil (a highly spiritual oil that can induce a meditative state) by rubbing just a single drop all over the surface of the crystal. Place the anointed crystal on your third eye, the energy center for which is located on your forehead between your eyes (taking great care with the oil to ensure you don't get any in or near your eyes).

2 Now, close your eyes. (This is a symbolic act that allows your third eye more freedom to open and your brain to more easily be able to discern between your invisible third eye and your physical eyes). Then repeat the following spell three times aloud:

MY THIRD EYE IS OPEN,
AN ALL-SEEING VIEW.
MY THIRD EYE WILL
SHOW WHAT MY HEART
KNOWS IS TRUE.

3 Now visualize a beautiful, bright, glowing eye in the center of your forehead. Envision several cords growing out of it—one that leads to your heart, one that leads straight into the earth, and one that reaches up toward the sky, stretching to an infinite height. At this point, you may remove the quartz from your forehead if you feel it is getting in the way of your third eye's energy; you may place it over your heart instead or hold it in your hand. Visualize your third eye in a literal way, as if you're somehow seeing a video of yourself at this very moment. Both eyes are closed, but a third eye on your forehead opens; an eye that connects straight to your heart and brain is opening wide. Pay attention to any feelings that come up or any additional visions you see. Repeat this spell any time you need to clear the pathway to your intuition.

HOW TO SPEAK WITCH

Throughout this book, I'll provide you with spells, each of which includes words for you to speak aloud. You can recite these spells word for word if they resonate with you. However, you might find that your spells feel even more powerful when you speak from your heart and write them yourself, even if that simply involves adding a few words here or there to the spell. This will become especially true as you further develop and learn to trust in your own intuition. While certain words, symbols, or elements certainly carry power in and of themselves (whether we ascribe them power or not), the bulk of the meaning in personal magick comes from you and the energy *you* bring to it.

So don't feel bound to the words in the pre-written spells in this book. They are powerful as-is, for sure, but I give you permission to change and tweak them for use in your private, personal practice so that they feel right for you. The more you feel the words in your heart, the more effective your spell will be.

WRITING YOUR OWN SPELLS

Because of the power of words, we should be selective and intentional with them when using them in spells. There are three key guidelines to making your spells most effective:

- **Be specific.**
- **Be positive.**
- **Be empowered.**

Take whatever comes to your mind, but be sure to tweak it according to these principles. You may need to change some words, add some words, or switch up the sentence structure—and that's okay. If you follow these guidelines, you'll be golden.

- **Be specific.** Trust and believe from my personal experience (and that of many other witches) that specificity is actually *really* important. Intention is wonderful, and we need that in order to drive our spells. But words themselves are powerful tools, which once we put them out into the world (by writing them down or speaking them aloud), gain the freedom to comingle and alchemize with other energies. And thus, the meaning of our intention must stand on its own. Be as specific as you can with your words. If there's a job you're going after, don't just refer to it as "the job I applied for" in your spell. State the job title, the responsibilities you'll have, the *details* that make it real and unmistakable from any other job. If there's an apartment you have your eye on, don't just name it as "that apartment" in your spell. Speak the address and the apartment number so there's absolutely no confusion. The universe listens to us, but we must make sure that we're offering up clear directions. This gives us the best chance of getting our desired outcome.

A LESSON ON BEING SPECIFIC

A psychic medium I know once shared a story about a love spell she conducted. She'd recently gotten out of a complicated relationship and did a spell opening herself up to new love. In it, she noted that she wanted to be with someone who "didn't have baggage." Soon after, she met and deeply connected with someone who'd just come into town, and as it turns out, he had virtually no belongings with him or in other words, no baggage. The universe has one twisted sense of humor, doesn't she? Of course, the intention behind her spell was to meet someone with no emotional baggage, given the complicated nature of her last relationship. So the spell worked—just a little differently than she'd intended.

- **Be positive.** When we conduct a spell, we obviously want it to go our way, so using positive language to state our intentions is necessary. In other words, try to speak in the affirmative. Instead of describing things you *don't* want, describe the things you *do* want. For example, if you're working a spell to boost your confidence, *don't* state something like "I no longer feel sh*tty and low about myself." Instead, say "I feel good about and confident in myself." Look at the difference in the words: The first sentence uses the word "sh*tty" and "low." The second sentence uses the words "good" and "confident." Remember, words have an inherent power. Use the ones that bring about the most positive, empowering feelings. Those are the key words that you want resonating in your spell (and that you want to subconsciously focus on); not the negative ones.

FAKE IT 'TIL YOU MAKE IT

You might feel self-conscious while saying certain spells aloud, or have inner doubts creep in and try to tell you the words aren't true. That's normal. Just tell that voice to f*ck right off. Keep repeating your intentions and mantras until you believe them. Your words have power—they can shape and change reality all around you, so they can obviously shape your mindset, too. Even if you have to repeat a mantra one hundred times before you get comfortable with it and start believing it, it's worth it. Don't stop.

- **Be empowered.** During a spell, you are trying to create a new reality. You're putting your intention into the universe, in the form of words and energy, and giving the universe a blueprint through which it can mirror this back to you in the form of reality. Thus, when you write your spells or list your intentions on paper, speak in the affirmative. This means stating your intentions as if they have already become reality or as if you are certain they will. So instead of saying you "want" something to happen, state that it *will* happen or *is* happening. Believe it. Model it. Own that sh*t. For example, say, "I am loved, supported, and attract people who inspire me and treat me with respect." Perhaps you don't actually feel that way in the moment (which is why you're working a spell to change it), but you'll want to state it that way anyway. Not only will making statements like this aloud strengthen your spell, but it will also empower you by making *you* believe it. Speaking your intentions can help you become more comfortable with the reality you're trying to create, which will allow the new circumstances to flow into your reality more easily. You're making space within yourself for the spell to work its magic.

CHAPTER 3

YOUR WITCHY TOOL BOX

IT'S TOOL TIME—WITCH STYLE. LET'S GET TO KNOW SOME OF THE STANDARD TOOLS OF THE TRADE.

Witchcraft is just more fun when you can play with the energy of different objects, concepts, trinkets, and treasures that bring a lil' something extra to your spells. Plus, who doesn't want an excuse to collect pretty crystals, candles, tarot decks, and bottles full of aromatic herbs?

THERE'S NO ONE RIGHT WAY TO BE A WITCH or to

cast spells. The possibilities are endless, and so are the types of tools you can choose from to make your spells more magickal. Just like you might love pop music while your best friend is all about punk, one witch can differ from the next in their spell and ritual style. How do you know which tools are right for you? Well, a huge part of witchcraft is getting in touch with your own intuition and deciding what *feels* right. This book will help you get better at learning how to listen to your inner voice—'cause that b*tch deserves to be heard, too!

Let's talk witchy tools. The first time I entered an occult shop—an entire room full of glittering pendulums, ornate incense burners, sparkling crystals, colorful tarot decks, and dozens of candles in jars—I felt like I did on my first trip to Disneyland. I didn't yet know what to *do* with any of it, but I knew I wanted to explore it.

Some of the tools that you will use in your spiritual practice and your spells are literal objects, while others are more conceptual in nature. Let's start with a couple of the helpful energies in the witchcraft world—deities and elements—as these are accessible to *everyone* and don't require money *or* storage space.

WORKING WITH DEITIES

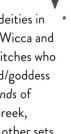

Many witches choose to work with various gods, goddesses, or other deities in their spells and spiritual practice (this is true for people who practice Wicca and many other witchcraft-based religions, but also for more "eclectic" witches who don't identify with any particular belief system). These archetypal god/goddess characters have been floatin' around human consciousness for *thousands* of years. You probably learned something about the deities of ancient Greek, Roman, and Egyptian cultures in school (although similar figures and other sets of deities exist in cultures all around the world). Some people worship deities as individual divine entities, while others simply call upon their archetypal qualities as a tool for their magick and personal growth. Others simplify things by calling on the divine feminine power of the Goddess and the divine masculine power of the God.

In addition to the gods 'n goddesses of the universe, some people also enjoy working with deities such as angels, saints, or elementals (which are the mystical beings of nature, such as fairies, gnomes, or elves). Sound kooky? Not all deities are for everyone. Believing in deities isn't a necessary part of doing spells and rituals, but it could certainly help to deepen your practice if you so choose.

If working with deities speaks to you, start learning more about it. There are lots of rituals that can be used to connect with and honor various deities, and you can call on their energy to aid you in your spells. It can also be helpful to simply meditate and open your heart to see if any archetypal figures or signs come forth. Then, based on the images you receive, try to figure out what deity it might be. Just don't forget to thank them and leave them an offering if you ask for their help!

WORKING WITH ELEMENTS

You can also call upon and work with elements to enhance your spells. The four main elements (air, earth, fire, and water) are the building blocks of life on our planet, and their energy plays a significant role in many sects of witchcraft. Elements appear in many different esoteric modalities, and each one corresponds with specific concepts and ideas. For example, each of the four suits in the tarot is associated with an element, just as each of the four elemental triplicities divide the zodiac signs. Even the four cardinal directions (north, south, east, and west) correspond with the energy of each of the four elements. The elements are also associated with different qualities within ourselves (which we'll discuss more below). We can use any and all of these correspondences symbolically in our spells.

There's also the fifth element that some people choose to incorporate into their practice, which is *spirit*—a more all-encompassing element that connects them all into one higher power.

In many forms of witchcraft, it's common to have an item to represent and honor each element on your altar or in your ritual workspace. It's also common to call upon the four elements before performing a spell or ritual (instructions on how to do that are in Chapter 4).

LET'S MEET THE ELEMENTS THAT CAN GUIC YOU IN CONNECTING WITH THE ALL-POWEF FORCES OF NATURE:

EARTH: Earth energy relates to the physical and material realm. It's our connection to nature, our physical senses, our sense of materialism, and the indulgence of our pleasures. The earth nourishes the body, and its energy makes us feel grounded, centered, and present in our physical bodies and sensations. Embrace the energy of earth in spells to feel grounded or to manifest money or material wealth and security. Earth is the element that makes our dreams and desires tangible. Some symbolic objects that represent the earth are, unsurprisingly, things that are derived from the earth: Plants, rocks, dirt, and herbs.

Correspondences:

- **Tarot** = Pentacles
- **Astrology signs** = Taurus, Virgo, Capricorn
- **Direction** = North

AIR: Air energy relates to our thoughts, mental powers, and ability to communicate. It's the oxygen we rhythmically breathe, in and out—lightweight, invisible, but essential. Air is the element that forms our desires into words. It's the only element we can't see with our eyes, which explains why it's associated with our *thoughts* and *ideas*. Doing breathwork or inhaling the fresh air of nature is a great way to channel air energy, as is using your mental powers to do a visualization. Embrace air energy in spells relating to seeking knowledge, generating ideas, or gaining mental clarity. Symbolic tools that represent air include things like feathers (think birds in the sky), smoke, or even the scent of diffused oils. Traditionally, swords and knives (or *athames*, as they're called in the witchy world) also represent the element of air.

Correspondences:

- **Tarot** = Swords
- **Astrology signs** = Gemini, Libra, Aquarius
- **Direction** = East

FIRE: Fire energy relates to our passion, creativity, and ability to take action. Just like fire itself, this energy is *hot*—it's the element that makes up the life-giving sun in the sky, which brings both light and warmth, and allows for all life on earth to exist. Fire is the spark that begets our desires. Embrace fire energy by lighting a candle or absorbing the warmth of the sun. Use it for spells that involve taking initiative on something, channeling creativity or passion, or fostering transformation. And as you can easily guess, fire is symbolically represented by fire! Candle magick is one very powerful way to invoke this element. Traditionally, wands are known to represent the element of fire.

Correspondences:

- **Tarot** = Wands
- **Astrology signs** = Aries, Leo, Sagittarius
- **Direction** = South

WATER: Water energy relates to our emotions, feelings, and intuition. Free-flowing and fluid, this element captures the essence of life. After all, life on earth *began* in water, and our bodies are largely made up of it! Water is the element that gives our intentions and desires a feeling and a longing. You can connect with water by taking a cleansing ritual bath, tracking and honoring the cycles of the moon (the moon rules water), or even having a soothing and cathartic cry session. Embrace the element of water when doing spells related to love, emotions, or even intuitive or psychic senses. Some symbolic objects that can be used to bring water energy to a spell are cups and chalices, herbal teas, or any sort of holy waters.

Correspondences:

- **Tarot** = Cups
- **Astrology signs** = Cancer, Scorpio, Pisces
- **Direction** = West

THE WITCH-SSENTIALS: THREE ULTRA-HELPFUL TOOLS

As you embark on your witchy path, there are a few key tools that will come in handy when it comes to making spell work more personal and powerful. These are a book of shadows, sigils, and an altar. While you certainly can go rogue and practice witchcraft free of these *witch-ssentials*, you might find that they help you develop a stronger relationship with your practice, and help make your spells even more unique and effective. That's the magic of magick: There's no one right way to do things, so pick and choose what works for you!

1 THE BOOK OF SHADOWS, A.K.A. YOUR WITCHY LIL' BLACK BOOK

Keeping track of your spells, rituals, and witchy explorations by writing them down in a special book is a really good way to stay on top of your sh*t. Think of this as a witchy diary or journal, except a hell of a lot more interesting because it's full of your "magick" instead of a bunch of dramatic recollections of convos with your crush (although we love those, too). A book like this is traditionally called a "grimoire" or a "book of shadows," but you can call yours whatever you please.

A book of shadows is a place to document the different spells and rituals you perform, keep track of your witchy knowledge and interests, and jot down anything else that you feel would aid your spells or strengthen your connection to your practice. This is your completely unique, one-of-a-kind, one-stop-shop for witchy info that's totally tailored to your experience and interest. And it's always a work in progress. Much like a diary, the end result is for your eyes only—so there's no reason to be self-conscious or edit yourself when it comes to deciding what to include.

WITCH TIP: A VIRTUAL BOOK OF SHADOWS

While some people prefer to have a physical book or journal that they can hold in their hands and fill with their own handwriting, it's totally legit to create a virtual book of shadows, too. So if you're more of a web witch, go ahead and open up a new document or a make an account with an online journal site and work your magick there instead.

BOOK OF SHADOWS SPELL

○ ☽ ☽ ☽ ☽ ☽ ● ☾ ☾ ☾ ☾ ○

STARTING YOUR BOOK OF SHADOWS IS A SPECIAL AND
NOTABLE NEW VENTURE. This spell makes a ritual out of it to add a little
more magick to the experience and make it "official."

GET IT TOGETHER

A few sticks of incense (*any scent*)

Your new book of shadows

Decorations for the book

(*image cutouts, dried flowers, rhinestones, colorful thread, glue or
Mod Podge—anything that will make the book cover your own*)

Nice pen

---

1 Set the mood and draw in some
energy for your ritual by lighting
a stick of incense. Now infuse your
book of shadows with your unique
brand of creativity by spending some
time decorating the book as you
see fit. You might want to cover the
outside of it in glittering rhinestones
or perhaps collage some inspiringly
witchy images on the front. Or
maybe just use a nice paint pen to
adorn the cover with a simple title.

2 Once you've made this witchy
tool your own, write your name
and your book's title inside the first
page, and set an intention for it.
This intention can be anything you
want! Don't overthink it—simply put
your goal for the book into your own
words, and write it down on a page.
Once that's complete, take your stick
of incense and move it in a clockwise
circle around the book in order to
cleanse and charge it. Now say the
following spell aloud:

**TONIGHT I BEGIN A
JOURNEY OF MAGIC.
I WRITE, I CREATE, I SHARE.
AS PAGES FILL, MY
KNOWLEDGE GROWS,
AND MAGICK TAKES ME THERE.**

3 Allow your incense stick to burn out safely. You're now ready to use your book of shadows.

HERE ARE TIPS ON HOW TO USE YOUR BOOK OF SHADOWS AND WAYS TO MAKE IT YOUR OWN.

- **Document the spells and rituals you perform, and writes notes about the results.** Write down what you did, when you did it, why, and how you chose it. Like, was it a keeper or did you lowkey hate it? This is perhaps the most important function of your witch diary: After you've been at it for a while, you'll have a whole book full of spells and rituals that you've actually used, so you'll be able to see exactly how useful they were. Take note of any visions that came to you, any energies you felt present, or any other details about how you felt as you performed the ritual. Include images, sensations, feelings, or even intrusive thoughts. Don't forget to leave space to write follow-up notes about the results of the spell so you know how effective it was later on!

- **Make notes on different types of magical tools and correspondences.** This includes tools you've tried working with and tools that you'd *like* to work with. Compile your witchy knowledge as you gain experience and do research. Drawn to candle magic? Google away, then make a list of what each different color candle represents so you don't have to look it up every time. Find yourself getting into astrology? Draw the zodiac wheel in your book of shadows, then list qualities of the signs' and planets' energies so that you can start planning rituals accordingly. And don't feel like you have to wait until you know *everything* about a particular tool to write about it— add it as you go along!

- **Use it as a spiritual journal.** While you may not want to use your book of shadows for everyday diary fodder, it may be useful to journal about any notable spiritual or symbolic experiences you've had. For example, maybe you had an especially epic lucid dream that was full of wild symbolism that you'd like to explore. Or perhaps you experienced some strange and magical coincidences that felt like a sign you were on the right path (or a hint that the results of a spell were beginning to take form). It's not always easy to remember the little details of our regular conversations, let alone the symbolic and esoteric moments we share with the universe. So be sure to jot down anything special that you'd like to recall and reference later on.

2 SIGILS, A.K.A. YOUR WITCHY SET OF EMOJIS

Connecting to symbolism is a *must* when it comes to casting spells and performing rituals. Objects are used as symbols in ritual work to represent larger themes and serve as conduits for energy. Using symbols called sigils and developing your own language with the energies you work with is another way to add fun and meaning to your practice.

You already have deep relationships with symbols in your everyday life, whether you realize it or not. Do you believe in luck? If so, perhaps you feel a little thrill when you find a heads-up penny on the ground or if you catch 11:11 on the clock, because you associate these things with good luck. Or conversely, perhaps you avoid walking underneath ladders or feel uneasy when you see a black cat for fear of *bad* luck. These are symbols—they may not have power in and of themselves, but it's the *meaning* we attribute to them that makes them powerful. A heads-up penny is just a piece of metal that fell on the ground, right? But to you, finding such a coin on the street could turn your whole day around.

Words are symbols, too. They represent our thoughts, feelings, desires. We use words in order to convey what's inside of us. And hello, *emojis*! These are symbols we all use every day; you and your closest crew likely share some emoji-based inside jokes. So there you have it: You already work with symbols in your daily life. Now you're just going to become more aware of them, use them with intention—and in the case of sigils—create some new ones.

Sigils are unique visual symbols or glyphs that represent concepts or beliefs. For example, this symbol:  represents release. You can draw sigils on your belongings to infuse them with magick, carve them into candles for a spell, or add them anywhere you want to add a layer of meaning. A quick Google search will reveal all sorts of sigils that others have created. You'll see that some are ancient as dust, while others have probably been created within the past twenty-four hours and immediately uploaded to social media (oh, the joys of being a modern-day witch!).

Looking up sigils for spells can be useful, but it can be even more exciting to create your *own* set of sigils to use in your spells. You can create these symbols for all different topics—a love sigil, money sigil, confidence sigil, energy sigil, calm sigil, creativity sigil. It's totally up to you.

WITCH TIP: DIY SECRET SIGILS

One cool way to create a sigil is by writing out your intention in a simple sentence, crossing out all the vowels and any double consonants, and then mixing up the remaining letters to create a symbol. For example, an intention such as "I will attract a supportive lover," can boil down to "wllttrctspprtvlvr," which will then become "wltrcspv" after canceling out the repeat consonants. You can blend those final remaining letters into a single symbol, like this:

You can also just draw inspiration from common cultural symbols (some easy examples would include a heart for love or a dollar sign for money) or by doing a meditation and seeing what comes to you, then working out the kinks until it looks right. Let yourself be inspired by other sigils or start from scratch. Here's a handy ritual to help inspire you to generate and ordain a custom sigil.

SIGIL-SEALING RITUAL

○ ☽ ☽ ❱ ❱ ❱ ● ● ❰ ❰ ❰❰ ❰ ○

THIS SPELL WILL HELP YOU CREATE AND THEN ACTIVATE YOUR OWN SIGIL. It's a rad way to put a unique spin on your own personal brand of magick. How cool is it to create a powerful and one-of-a-kind symbol that you can use in your spells for years to come?

GET IT TOGETHER

1 orange candle (*to represent creativity*)

Paper and pen or marker

Music, incense, or any other sensory triggers that embody the energy of the sigil you're creating

1 Before you begin your ritual, you'll need to figure out exactly what you'd like your new sigil to represent. Write it down in a few clear, concise words, or in the form of a brief and affirmative statement. Now close your eyes and allow yourself to think about all the associations you have with the concept your sigil will represent, whether it's love, money, protection, good luck, or anything else. As you create your sigil, you'll want to evoke that energy for inspiration and clarity.

For example, if the sigil is for confidence, perhaps there are some empowering anthems that always make you feel good while you listen to them—so throw those onto a playlist to listen to while you create. If the sigil is for love and you know the smell of roses always gets you feeling romantic, burn a rose-scented candle, light some rose incense, or diffuse some rose essential oil to get you in the mood. You get the picture.

2 Now set your sigil-creatin' scene! Light the orange candle as an offering to the muse of inspiration and to symbolize your creative energy burning brightly. Then incorporate whatever sensually inspiring additions you chose to help you get focused—put on the playlist, light the incense, or wear the accessories or clothes that help you get in the zone. Get out your pen or marker and paper: It's time to create.

3 Start your creative process by drawing symbols that you already associate with your concept. For example, draw hearts for love, dollar signs for money, smiley faces for happiness, etc. These basic shapes and symbols could serve as a starting point or inspiration for a new symbol of your own creation. But don't feel bound to this—you can make your sigil look however you want. You can also use the method described in the DIY Secret Sigil witch tip on page 42 where you write an intention, cross out vowels and double letters, and turn the remaining letters into a unique sigil.

4 No matter what route you take, once your sigil starts taking form (and you'll know it), keep working with it until it's as clean, simple, and intentional as possible. Every line, curve, and stroke should be thought out and consciously considered. Keep in mind that there's usually an element of simplicity to a sigil. After all, the idea is that you can use it repeatedly and hopefully recreate it with some level of ease. So don't rush it. Work with it, redo it, refine it, and tweak it until it looks and feels *right*.

5 Once your sigil is completed, draw it into your book of shadows along with your intention. Incorporate it into spells by drawing it on paper, carving it into a candle, or otherwise mirroring its imagery. You may also draw the sigil on a piece of paper and then burn it to simply put the intention out into the universe without any additional elements.

3 THE ALTAR, A.K.A. YOUR WITCHY WORKSPACE

In the witch world, altars are a unique and sacred space in your home where you can cast your spells and rituals, honor your spiritual guides or ancestors, and display your witchy tools. I mean, honestly, you can do your rituals on your bedroom floor, at your kitchen table, in your backyard—wherever the f*ck you want to! But having a designated witchy work space can make your spell casting (and your everyday life) feel extra magical.

Altars also offer an easy way for you to honor any "divine powers" that you believe in (whether that's a god or goddess, or just your higher self). They're often redecorated as the seasons change, which helps you connect with the earth's natural cycles. This might sound like serious spiritual business, but creating and maintaining an altar is actually surprisingly fun. It's basically a tangible and interactive spiritual mood board that represents your one-of-a-kind connection and witchy practice.

You can create your altar anywhere—on a dresser or tabletop, on a shelf, or even atop an overturned box. There are guidelines and suggestions for what to include on an altar (which are listed on the following pages), but there are no rules, and yours can be whatever you want it to be. While there may be some items that you always keep on your altar (like certain candles, crystals, and other mystical tools), it's also normal to switch up the symbolic objects you display there on the regular. For example, if you're working on upping your confidence and planning spells related to that, put a hot photo of yourself up on your altar along with a mirror to show you your beautiful face every time you get spiritual. If you're trying to make it rain and manifest some extra cash, put literal money and other materially valuable objects on your altar. Your altar can reflect elements of *anything* you're trying to bring into your life through magic.

And don't forget about the *cute* factor! If you're going to have an altar in your room or home, then obviously you want it to jive with your overall decorative vibe. Just because it's a "sacred space" doesn't mean it can't be adorable, fun, and totally synced with your personal aesthetic. Make it your own in all the ways you can by using colors, materials, and objects that scream *you*. Want to display a photo on your altar? Put it in a cute frame that matches your decor. Setting out some fresh flowers as an offering? Use a funky vase that you love looking at. Your sacred, special space should make you feel happy, excited, and totally yourself. If it doesn't feel authentically you, then f*ck it—make your own rules.

Do you *need* an altar in order to do spells? Absolutely not! You can do your spells and rituals anywhere you feel comfortable. But having an altar can certainly be helpful, as it can help make magick and spirituality part of your everyday life in an easy, cute, and aesthetic way. Plus, can we just note how incredibly witchy you will feel with a freaking *altar* set up in your room?

Building an altar can be intimidating, but don't stress out, because there's no one right way to do it. It can be big or small, colorful or subtle, hidden in the closet or the main focus of a room. What's important is that your altar reflects your relationship to the universe; put anything that inspires you to get deep with yourself and connect with the natural cycles and mysteries of life. Here are some ideas for things to display on your altar:

- **Something to represent each element.** Not that you have to follow anyone else's rules, but it's traditional to represent the four elements on your altar, which are air, earth, fire, and water. Any object that channels the energy of a particular element for you is all you need to find, but there are some typical correspondences that can help. For air, you could use the smoke of a stick of incense or a feather (to represent a bird flying through the skies). Earth is easy—you could use a potted plant, a crystal, or any other natural objects that are meaningful to you. Fire is another easy one; as you guessed it, candles are always a solid bet here. And for water, you could use a witchy chalice or a little bottle of healing water.

- **Your magical tools & supplies.** An altar can double as a *very* cute storage area for all your magical supplies. Keep your tools of the trade displayed here for easy access. Set out your crystals, keep your deck of tarot cards here, and display your candles. Keeping your magical tools on your altar isn't just convenient for when it comes to casting your spells, it's also helpful to keep these tools alongside other sentimental and symbolic objects, as it helps to infuse them with the magick of your practice.

- **Sentimental objects that boost and honor your spiritual connection.** Everyone has different things that are meaningful to them, so your altar might include some unique and funky objects, too. For example, you may want to honor loved ones who have passed with photos or mementos, or you may have other little objects that you hold sacred for other reasons (like trinkets from your childhood or other sentimental gifts).

- **An offering to whatever higher power you believe in (even if that's just your higher self!).** It's always helpful to keep an offering or two on your altar, too, as a symbolic gesture of gratitude to the universe for working with you. You could set out some fruit, pour a bit of wine in a nice chalice, or put out a vase of fresh flowers. Whatever you choose, make sure you switch things out and keep everything fresh and clean—you don't want drooping flowers or rotting fruit mucking up your sacred space!

- **Symbols for the changing season.** Altars are often used as part of traditional rituals to honor the witchy holidays (also known as sabbats in the pagan and Wiccan world), and these coincide with the changing of the seasons. Whether or not you celebrate these holidays, acknowledging the changing seasons is a great way to ground yourself and get connected with the earth's natural cycles—which are all too easy to ignore in our

WITCH TIP: ALTAR ON THE GO

Having an altar in a nice, chill place in your home can be a sanctuary for when it comes time to do a spell—but we're a buncha busy witches, so we can't always plan around that. Having a little "altar on the go" is a great way to ensure you stay up on your magical practice even when you're out of town or on your way somewhere!

Get a small wooden box or satchel and fill it with small items to represent each of the four main elements, like a tea light candle for fire (don't forget a pack of matches or a small lighter), an incense cone for air, a mini-bottle of rose water for water, and a small pocket-sized crystal for earth. Include some sort of small, pretty cloth or fabric that can be folded up inside your box or bag; use this to lay over any surface to create your little sacred workspace. It could be anything from a lace doily to a silky neck scarf! Feel free to add anything else that speaks to you, and call it a day.

Now you've got a miniature altar-on-the-go that you can throw in your bag anytime you're taking a trip or planning a simple spell or ritual outside the house.

fast-paced and high-tech world. Your altar can easily reflect the time of the year with symbolic objects like seeds for spring, sunflowers for summer, pumpkins for autumn, and candles for winter.

Try the Altar + Control + Delete Restart Ritual if you've got an altar you want to freshen the vibes on, or if you're just creating one from scratch.

ALTAR + CTRL + DELETE RESTART RITUAL

○ ☽ ☽ ☽ ☽ ● ● ● ☾ ☾ ☾ ○

AN ALTAR NEEDS TO BE MAINTAINED IN ORDER TO BE
EFFECTIVE. That means cleaning it often, changing the arrangement of
your treasured objects to keep things feeling fresh, and making sure that any
offerings (plants, food, candles, etc.) are being switched out regularly. It's also
important to make sure the energy of your altar is in balance! If you feel like
your altar needs a nice deep cleanse, this altar restart ritual will break up any
stagnant energy and help you spruce things up. If you're creating your altar for
the first time, this is also a great way to turn that process into a ritual and infuse
it with some magic.

GET IT TOGETHER

Cleansing water
*(you can use a product like Florida water, or simply use
some water mixed with sea salt instead)*

Small rag or cloth for cleaning

1 item to represent each of the four elements *(earth, air, fire, water)*

Fresh offerings *(such as fruit, flowers, food, or wine)*

Smoke cleanser tool *(like bundled sage, lavender, or incense)*

1 If you already have an altar, begin
the ritual by acknowledging it
in its current state and thanking
your guides or higher self for the
support it has offered. Now clap your
hands loudly as you move them in a
clockwise circle around the perimeter
of the altar. The loud sound of the
clap helps to break up the energy
surrounding your altar and get it
moving before you start moving the
physical objects themselves!

2 The first step will be removing anything from the altar that is stagnant or used. Things like burnt-down candles, incense stubs, wilting flowers, or ripened fruit should be removed and either thrown away, buried outdoors (which is fine for compostable items, like plants or food), or reused in some way. For example, it's totally okay to eat fruit from your altar once it's fully ripened, because the universe doesn't want you to waste perfectly good food. You could also hang-dry your fresh flowers to create beautiful decorative pieces that are also symbolic to your witchy practice.

3 Now begin the process of removing the remaining objects one by one from the altar. As you pick up each item, think of its place and significance on your altar and thank it for its energy. You may speak the following spell aloud to each item as you express your gratitude:

AS A TOOL AND A FRIEND, YOUR SERVICE TRANSCENDS, AND I THANK YOU FOR THE ENERGY THAT YOU SEND.

4 Once your altar is clear of its adornments, clean the surface by dampening a rag with a bit of cleansing water, or Florida water, if using (Florida water is a liquid containing alcohol that is highly cleansing, which also contains several different plant oils with spiritual properties).

5 Now it's time to rebuild your altar. Begin with the items that represent the four elements. Feel the object's spiritual and physical forms being cleansed and take a moment to mentally connect with the element it represents before putting it in its place on the altar.

6 Once you've got the elements represented, move on to the other objects you'd like to include. Piece by piece, hold the object in your hands and gently clean it off using cleansing water or Florida water if needed. **(Safety note: If you clean off candles or any other objects with Florida water, wait until everything is FULLY dry before you light an open flame, as this water is highly flammable when wet.)** Connect with it; what is it telling you? Does it want to be part of your altar? Do you still truly want it to be part of your altar? Sometimes we might include things out of habit without listening to our intuition, so make sure each item is one that really feels right. You want your altar to be as well curated as possible for maximum potency! Repeat this process with each item until you've rebuilt your altar.

7 As the final step of this ritual, you will set out an offering to whatever higher power you believe in (which simply could be the divine spirit within you or your higher self). You may put out whatever offering you're vibin', such as fruit or some other type of food, fresh flowers, or a glass of wine or some other drink. As you set out the offering and close your ritual, say the following spell aloud:

> **A PLACE TO HONOR,**
> **A SPACE TO SEE**
> **AN ALTAR THAT SHOWS**
> **THE REFLECTION OF ME.**
> **A PLACE TO EXPLORE,**
> **A SPACE TO PLAY**
> **CONNECTING WITH**
> **MAGICK EVERY DAY.**

Your spell is complete, and your altar is officially cleansed and refreshed!

THE ENCHANTED TOOLS OF THE TRADE

It's finally tool time, witches. Perhaps one of the most irresistible aspects of witch life is the mystical 'n magickal tools of the witchy trade. Whether it's crystals, wands, or little jars full of herbs and sparkles, these ritualistic items add tons of quirk and flair to the mystique of witchcraft.

It's easy to be enchanted by the magick and beauty of mystical tools, but they serve a much greater purpose. Each of these tools have different spiritual meanings and uses, and they can help you drum up energy for a spell as well as connect with the natural elements all around you. While having many tools isn't required to cast effective spells, it can certainly be a powerful (and let's face it, *fun*) part of your witchy practice.

Don't feel like you have to go out and acquire all or any of these items or skills at once (or ever). Your spells can be just as rich and effective if all you use are items you already have in your home! Many witches have just a few reliable tools that they work with regularly in their personal witch arsenal. Perhaps for you, those are simply the herbs from your kitchen and some candles you dug out of a drawer. No biggie! It's totally up to you what you use in spells and what you don't.

Use your intuition when it comes to picking your magical tools. We don't always have to follow our analytical brain; this is supposed to be fun, so loosen up! If you want to branch out and try some new things, seek whatever items you feel energetically called to connect with. And no rush to learn everything about *all* the things, *all* at once—it's better to introduce new tools into your practice slowly, so that you can take your time forming relationships with them. It's important that when you acquire a new tool, you take some time to *vibe* with it. Get to know its energy.

Virtually *anything* or *nothing* can be used in a ritual, y'all, but here's a quick tour of some of the popular mystical tools that you might come across during your witchy explorations (and may want to try out for yourself). Some are used more traditionally, while other are more popular in the modern-day craft:

ATHAME: This isn't your mother's kitchen knife, kids. "Athame" is a fancy word for a knife, typically with a black handle, that's used ceremonially in spells and rituals—but no, we're not getting weird and drawing blood! In fact, athames are *never* used to cut anyone's skin. Many aren't even made to be sharp enough to cut through anything tangible (it's a magickal tool, not a weapon!). Rather, athames are used symbolically to "cut ties" or direct energy during a spell. It's a staple in more traditional practices, but not everyone feels comfy using these in rituals of their own, and that's fine. Athames are commonly associated with the element of air (just as swords are in the tarot) but they're sometimes associated with fire, too.

CUP OR CHALICE: Cups (also called chalices or goblets, if you're feelin' fancy) are traditionally used on altars and in rituals, especially in Wicca. It can be used on your altar to represent the element of water, filled and set out as an offering, or used in spells that require you to drink something or symbolically set out an empty glass.

WITCH TIP: KEEP IT SIMPLE

You don't have to get something special and witchy to serve as a tool—any cup or knife can serve as a chalice or athame. Just make sure whatever you use, you set it aside for the sole purpose of spells!

WAND: Stage magicians don't get to have all the fun—witches use magick wands too. Except they're not just for show. Wands can be used to direct energy in a spell. They don't need to be anything fancy. They're traditionally made out of wood or some other natural material.

For a free wand, use a nice piece of found wood, and draw symbols or sigils on the branch to make it extra magickal. You can even attach a crystal to the tip using twine or wire!

Speaking of crystals, you can use a crystal wand, too. Look for pieces that have a wand-like shape. Selenite is easy to find in long, wand-like sticks (as that's how it naturally grows) and it's very energetically powerful, making it great for this purpose.

BESOMS: Brooms aren't just for the witches on TV! They're actually a traditional tool used in witchcraft, although not for flying on as you cackle into the night. Just like a regular broom is used for cleaning up your house, a broom or besom in witchcraft, is used for *energetic* cleansing—like "sweeping" away bad vibes before a spell, or cleansing the energy throughout your house or room. Because of this, your ritual broom doesn't have to be chosen for its function, because it likely won't ever sweep a speck of dust! That means you could use a cute miniature or decorative broom, or even make one on your own.

CANDLES: Evoking the energy of fire, candles are a staple in many spells and rituals. They're powerful, easy to find, easy to use, and so versatile—you can anoint them with oils, carve symbols into them, and use different colors for different effects (as each color has a symbolic meaning in witchcraft).

There are a few different commonly used candles in witchcraft: small chime candles that burn in their entirety in a few hours; larger altar candles; and 7-day candles, which are typically enclosed in a tall glass jar (and are sometimes inscribed with symbols or prayers). That said, any candle will do, as the energy of the flame evokes the power of the element of fire and brings a bright and burning energy to any spell and intention, making them a witchy fan favorite.

CAULDRON: Here's another classic witch stereotype come to life—but again, it's not what you think, as we're not using a cauldron to cook up creepy potions made with animal bodies! Not everyone has room for (or money to spend on) a full-sized cast-iron cauldron, so many witches use a cute mini-cauldron for their witchy work. So long as your cauldron is fireproof, it can be used as a safe place to burn papers, small candles, or herbs during a spell. It can also be used to mix spell ingredients together or hold liquids. You can also use a firesafe bowl for a similar purpose, if you haven't gotten your hands on a legit cauldron.

CRYSTALS: Glorified rocks or magical conduits of energy? Trick question, because crystals are *both*. Many witches believe that crystals have energies, and that our personal frequency can align with theirs. Every crystal has different purported metaphysical properties, which is why certain rituals call for certain stones. Crystals can also be charged with your personal intentions, which can make them very useful in spell work. Crystals can be used to connect with the energy of the earth and represent the element of earth on an altar.

WITCH TIP: BE A CRYSTAL WHISPERER

There's no need to do hours of research on what crystals mean before going out to buy one. Try to trust your gut and listen to which crystals call out to you as you're choosing one. You'll often find that your intuition will lead you to exactly the piece you needed to help boost your confidence, calm your nerves, attract your crush, or do whatever else you had on your mystical wish list.

HERBS & PLANTS: We know herbs are tasty (shout-out to salads everywhere), and we also know they're powerful healing tools, believed to have all sorts of medicinal qualities—which is why people take them in vitamins, teas, or tinctures on the regular. But in addition to their health benefits, herbs, flowers, and other plants are believed to have many spiritual properties, too. Herbs and flowers (fresh or dried) are commonly used in rituals: They can be burned as cleansing agents, used to dress candles, or made into oils (like essential oils) that can be diffused or used to anoint things. Herbs and other plants generally correspond to the energy of the earth.

WITCH TIP: ALL HAIL ROSEMARY!

Rosemary is one of the best all-purpose herbs to keep in your witchy apothecary. And thankfully, it's easy to grow or find at any grocery store. Rosemary is known to attract love, bring luck in money, enhance the mind, and is commonly used for both cleansing and purifying. Plus, it's safe to ingest, burn as a smoke cleanser, or add to your bath water.

BELLS, CHIMES, OR SINGING BOWLS: Sound can be such an amazing and healing energy for magick! A classic tool in witchcraft, bells are often used to signify the beginning of a ritual or clear the energy after one. But they can be useful in all sorts of less-traditional rituals, too. The clear tone of a bell or chime breaks up energy and clears negativity using its sound frequency, as many people believe this sound can be healing and cleansing. You may also use it symbolically during spells and rituals to call in energy or signal the beginning and end of your spell.

MYSTICAL WATERS: There are all different types of waters that can be used in your rituals. A popular one is a product called "Florida water," which is a traditional blend of scented oils in alcohol that's beloved for its cleansing properties. You may also use salt water for cleansing. Moon water (water that's been charged under a full or new moon), rose water, sun-charged water, or collected rain or sea water can also be used effectively in spells and rituals.

SMOKE CLEANSING & CENSING TOOLS: Ceremonially burning incense, resins, oils, and bundles of dried herbs serves multiple functions in the witch world. First, because many smoke cleansers are made directly from plants (or based on the scent of them), they also carry the spiritual symbolism of the plant. So if you don't have a specific herb, leaf, or flower for a spell, you can sometimes substitute an incense or oil from the same plant instead; it can still bring forth the plant's energy and spiritual qualities for the ritual. And remember to be both culturally aware and ecologically conscious about the smoke cleansing tools you use and where you source them from—it is best to look for herbs that are harvested sustainably and locally, and that aren't appropriating someone else's culture.

Second, plant powers aside, the act of burning (or "censing") something to produce smoke can serve as a cleansing mechanism (you can move a lit stick of incense or bundle of herbs in a clockwise motion around something in order to cleanse its energy, using its smoke). Finally, the smoke produced by burning these censors can also be used to represent the element of air on your altar or in a spell.

OILS: Oils are often used in magick as a way to infuse spells and rituals with the energy of plants. You can use essential oils, which are highly concentrated plant oils, or you can make your own oils by infusing herbs in a carrier oil and letting them sit over a period of a couple weeks.

DIVINATION TOOLS & METHODS

Witches aren't necessarily psychic, but a big part of working spells and rituals involves getting in touch with your intuition. Strengthening that sense by using divination tools can help you get in touch with your all-seeing self. Divination tools refer to any system that can be used to offer insight into the future. They almost work as a liaison between your conscious mind and your intuition or the divine, depending on your beliefs. Here are a few common examples (although there are many others!):

Pendulum: A pendulum is a divination tool used to channel a divine higher power or just tap into your inner self (depending on what you believe!) in order to answer questions in a practice called "pendulum dowsing." Dowsing is typically used to answer *yes* or *no* questions; how the pendulum moves, rocks, or spins as the user holds it still and asks the question is its way of communicating.

Runes: Runes are a set of ancient symbols (similar to sigils) commonly used in spells and rituals, and sometimes used as another form of divination. You often work with runes in the form of rune stones, which can be used as a divination tool to answer questions or offer spiritual guidance in any given situation. The rune symbols can also be used like sigils and carved into candles or drawn on paper, if you want to call upon their energy during a spell or ritual.

Tarot and Oracle Cards: The tarot is a system of cards (divided into two sections: the major arcana and the minor arcana), each of which hold a different meaning and symbolism and are used for divination purposes. Many people use tarot cards in their spiritual practice as part of a ritual to gain insight or guidance into a situation, or to help answer a question. They're often drawn in the form of a spread, in which different positions of the cards represent different parts of someone's life or situation.

Oracle cards, commonly found in occult shops, are sort of like the less-intense and much more casual little sis' to the tarot. They're typically drawn one at a time rather than in a full spread, and often used to get a quick bit of guidance or a "vibe" on something. They can also be used to supplement a tarot spread if you're seeking additional insight into a particular card's meaning and placement.

Scrying: Scrying is the act of looking into something and interpreting what you see in order to answer questions, gain insight into a situation, or see into the future. You know the stereotype of a fortune teller looking into a crystal ball? Well, reflective crystal balls can actually be used for scrying purposes! Other forms of scrying include gazing at a flame or looking into a reflective surface or crystal and seeing what images appear to you. You may also fill a bowl or cauldron with water and scry into the liquid's reflection. This can take time to get comfortable with, as it can be difficult to interpret visualization and images when you're not used to doing so, but with some practice you may find scrying to be a helpful tool to incorporate in your magical workings.

WITCH TIP: BOND WITH YOUR TAROT CARDS

When you get a new deck of tarot or oracle cards, it's advised to sleep with the deck under your pillow for three nights before using it. This helps you subconsciously connect with the cards and energetically "claim" them.

WITCH ON A BUDGET

Believe it or not, you don't have to buy expensive tools to get sh*t done through your spells. There are plenty of spells and rituals that can be performed with inexpensive and easy-to-find tools and ingredients. In fact, many spells ask for ingredients that you might already have at home. Here are some helpful and creative tips for gathering supplies, especially for all of us witches on a budget.

- **Reuse, recycle, and repurpose.** Why go out and buy things when you can reuse what you've already got? Wash out and save glass food jars in different sizes to hold your herbs or homemade magickal oils, or to use as spell jars. If you have any tinctures, oils, or even pretty cosmetics bottles, clean and save those bottles when they've run out so you can use them to create your own oils or herbal blends. You can easily repurpose glass or tin candle holders, too. Get rid of excess wax in a candle container by putting it in the freezer and scraping it clean (the wax will flake off more easily that way).

- **Get crafty. *Witchcrafty.*** If you're a creative and resourceful witch, there's lots you can do. Make a magickal DIY candle by saving up the excess wax in older candle holders. When you have enough, heat the container to the wax's melting point, pour the leftover waxes into a new container with a fresh candle wick, and mix in some dried herbs or a few drops of scented oil. You can also do things like create your own pendulum with a magickal object and a string, or make your own magick wand by affixing a crystal onto the tip of a sturdy piece of wood. The possibilities are endless.

- **Raid your own pantry.** You likely have tons of herbs, spices, and teas in your kitchen *right now* that can easily be used in spells. Salt, for example, is highly purifying, and black pepper can dispel negativity. Sugar and other natural sweeteners can be used to "sweeten" a situation in a spell, and both bay leaves and dried sage are great to burn as smoke cleansers. Almost all herbs—even common ones like dill, rosemary, thyme, cinnamon, chamomile, and more—have useful mystical qualities and are often called for in spells. Check what you've already got, and look up their magickal properties (you'll find lots of standard kitchen herbs used in the spells throughout this book!).

HERBS	MAGICKAL PROPERTIES
Basil	Both purifying and protective. Brings abundance, money, and prosperity.
Bay laurel (bay leaves)	Powerful for manifesting and intention-setting. Burn leaves as a smoke cleanser to banish negative energy.
Black pepper	Protection against negativity and bad energy.
Chamomile	Calming and gentle; often used for meditation and relaxation, as well as luck in money.
Cinnamon	Brings heat, passion, and excitement in love; as well as healing and spirituality. Can be used to speed up spells.
Clove	Used for banishing gossip as well as making yourself more attractive in love and romance.
Peppermint	Used for cleansing energy and healing. Can be used in dream spells or sleep rituals.
Rosemary	Multi-purpose purifying herb that brings clarity of mind. Used in love, money, and protection spells alike.
Sage	Cleansing and healing. Also used to bring luck and prosperity when it comes to money.
Salt	A witch's must-have! Purifies and cleanses negative energies. Also used for protection and marking boundaries during rituals.
Vanilla	Brings sensuality, sweetness, and sexiness in love. Used to enhance attractiveness and passion.

- **Forage for supplies in nature.** So many natural objects serve as powerful tools for magick. Learn to identify herbs and flowers in your yard or near your home so that you can pick them when you come across them; look up the magickal properties of each so you can use them in spells as needed. You can even dry out flower petals and herbs at home for later use. For example, rose petals are easy to find, and they happen to be fabulous for love spells and attracting romance. Pick up dried eucalyptus leaves, seashells, pretty rocks, or feathers as you come upon them. Nature's treasures are a witch's best friend.

- **Hit the closest dollar store or food market.** There are plenty of witchy items that you can find at your local market or dollar store. Look for candles (there are usually 7-day candles, which are tall and poured into a glass cylinder, taper candles, and smaller candles) as well as cheap candle holders. You'll also likely be able to find all sorts of salts and dried herbs in the food section, as well as different types of herbal teas. Many dollar stores also carry incense sticks or oils. It is also a great place to purchase notebooks, glitter, pens, and other craft supplies, if you're looking to create some magickal crafts.

WITCH TIP: BAY LEAVES

Have bay leaves in your kitchen? These can be used in quick and effective manifestation or wishing spells, *and* for smoke cleansing. Write your intention on one and set it ablaze in a fireproof bowl in order to send your intention out into the universe, or simply burn one and allow the healing herbal smoke to cleanse your space.

- **Don't sleep on thrift stores.** Hitting thrift stores is a fantastic way to find really cool pieces on the cheap. Peep the home goods section and keep an eye out for cool witchy candle holders, athames, incense burners, or other items that can be worked into your spiritual practice or displayed on your altar. If you don't already have a chalice, I recommend checking thrift stores for funky ornate glassware or fancy wine goblets, too. Thrift stores are also great places to find old occult books if you're looking to learn more about a particular topic.

- **Spend your money wisely.** If you're going to splurge on buying something, make it count by investing in tools with a wide variety of uses. For example, stock up on some white candles, which can often be used in place of another color. And if you're just going to get a single crystal to start with, clear quartz is a good bet! Clear quartz has a very easy-to-work with and easy-to-vibe-with energy that amplifies virtually *any* intentions, so you can often use it in place of another crystal in a spell if you don't have the crystal that's suggested.

- **Don't be afraid to improvise.** Don't have a traditional spell candle? Use a regular one, even if you have to draw your sigil on the side of the candle holder instead of carving it into the wax. Have some patchouli incense but not the patchouli oil that a ritual calls for? Use the smoke from the incense as an anointing tool instead! Get creative. Unless the creator of a ritual notes that a particular ingredient cannot be subbed with something else for some important reason, then feel free to follow your intuition and use what you have.

CHAPTER 4

SPELL PREP
101

LIGHTS, CANDLES, ACTION—IT'S TIME TO SET THE STAGE FOR MAGICK

You're showered, dressed up, and feelin' good. You've cleaned up your room, lit some candles, and put on some mood music. No, you're not having a hot date over—you're prepping for an enchanting and effective ritual!

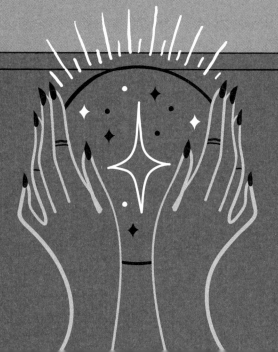

WHEN YOU PERFORM A SPELL OR A RITUAL, you're literally about to engage in an energetic exchange with the universe. This is a very cool thing! This is a very special thing! This is a very amazing thing! So treat it as such. This is not an ordinary, mundane moment of your day. It's a moment of magick between you and the energy around you, and thus it needs to be honored as the sparkly ceremony that it is.

But before we dive into exactly how to set the stage for a spell, let's answer this question: When you're working with spells, who are you working with?

LET'S TALK ABOUT HIGHER POWERS

First and foremost, when you do spiritual spells and rituals, you're working with yourself. This is deep and personal work; the power and energy that's put into a spell is *your own*. However, many people feel they're also working with and calling in a "higher power" of sorts, and that can charge a spell with even more power.

If you are already a spiritual person, you can totally incorporate your own notion of a higher power into your spells, regardless of what that looks like. You can call upon this power to help you in your spells, and pray to it for clarity. Throughout this book, I'll often refer to "the Universe" as an all-encompassing higher power of sorts. I feel that this infinite and ever-mysterious force that we exist *within* is the closest thing that we all share as an undeniable concept of mind-boggling higher intelligence. You can see it reflected in nature, in people, in the force of life itself. If you personally believe in a "higher power" but don't identify with the word "God," "Source," "Spirit," or other common terms, feel free to define it in whatever way feels best—Goddess, the Divine, the Universe, whatever works. Your spiritual connection is an energy source, so celebrate it and use it.

If you don't believe in any sort of higher power, that's fine, too. You can still work spells and rituals without that connection or belief system. If that's the case, it simply means that what you are calling forth during your spells and rituals is a different kind of energy—the energy of your *higher self* or the energy of the Universe—which makes life spring forth from the elements, which allows us (our biology, our ecology, everything) to work in such a divine and symbiotic fashion, which creates that feeling of interconnectedness with nature and each other. These are just as powerful sources of energy for your spells.

LET'S ALSO TALK ABOUT YOUR HIGHER SELF

When working with witchcraft, we develop a strong relationship with energy, and one of the things I mentioned in the introduction to this book is developing a relationship with the energy within *yourself*. Think of this as a form of *divine* energy within yourself—the Goddess within you. You can also think of this energy within you as your *higher self*. Your higher self *is* a higher power, so you don't have to believe in any sort of mystical, god-like figure to channel it.

Physically, your higher self is the mystical and mysterious intelligence within you that directs all the automatic functions of your body; it makes your heart beat, your wounds heal, your lungs breathe. On a more ethereal level, think of your higher self as your "sixth sense," which is the feeling of transcendence you might get when seeing something beautiful or experiencing deep love. We're all made of the same stuff—literally, stardust—so your higher self is simply that part of you that you can *trust*, the one who wants the best, the one who emerges when you're growing and taking the lead.

The only power you *need* to work with in order to make magick is your higher self. Your subconscious, your unconscious, your spirit, your inner, deeper, higher-vibration *you*. If you work magic, you're simply getting your higher self on board and strengthening your relationship. And if you want to think of this on a more literal level rather than a magickal one, you could say that by crystallizing your intentions into words, visualizing your desired reality, and performing a ritual to give even *more* energy to your desire is simply directing you toward all the right choices and the right opportunities in order to *create* that desired reality. And if that's the case, great! There is magick in that, too.

Now that you know who and what you're working with in a spell, it's time to learn all the steps to properly open and close a spell.

STEP 1: SETTING THE STAGE

Before you dive into a spell, you'll want to make sure the space around you is in the right shape to host this special event. Think of how you'd act if you were having a friend over from out of town. You'd likely want to clean up your space so it looked nice, right? You'd also want to clear your schedule to ensure no one else showed up that might take attention away from your date. You'd want to set a nice ambience—perhaps by making a chill playlist, preparing some drinks or snacks, and lighting a yummy-smelling candle.

This is exactly how you should treat your magick-making time, too. Clear your sched, do at least a quick pickup of your space, and set the ambience with whatever will get you into a high-vibe mindset.

- **Clean up your crap.** Don't be a lazy witch! Take a few minutes to tidy up your witchy workspace. If you have an altar, great—spruce that baby up and get it ready for your spell. If not, then decide where you'll be working your spell and make sure the area is clean, cleared of clutter and debris, and that spell ingredients are laid out and ready to go. You should also take a few minutes to make sure *you* feel confident, powerful, and sexy going into your spell casting. Perhaps you have an outfit that makes you feel particularly empowered, or maybe you want to do your spell totally naked. Do whatever makes you feel like the most powerful version of yourself.

- **Plan the right time and place.** For a spell to be effective, clear your mind and schedule of distractions before you begin in order to focus on the task at hand. Even if it's a quickie, energy work requires your full attention; if you half-ass your spell, you'll likely produce half-assed results, too! Plan your ritual in a space where you feel comfortable doing what's required, and where you won't be interrupted or distracted for the duration of the ritual. This means putting your phone on do not disturb for the time being (because let's be real, we can't *not* get distracted over whether or not that buzz was a notification from our crush).

STEP 2: CLEANSE, CLEANSE, CLEANSE

Okay, so we discussed making sure your witchy workspace is clean and clutter-free, right? Well, now, you also need to make sure the space is *energetically* cleansed (and that *your* energy is, too!). This is an absolute must-do practice for any witch or energy worker.

As we go about our day, we run into all sorts of germs, dirt, and grime. We sweat. We get dirty. But we also pick up all sorts of energy, emotional baggage, and spiritual dirt 'n grime as we go about our day, too, so it's important to cleanse *that* crap away! If your aura is grimy and gross, how can you expect to feel clear-sighted when it comes to your intuition? So before jumping into a spell, you'll want to cleanse your space to clear away any stagnant or unfamiliar energy that could detract from the power of your ritual. There are so many ways to cleanse yourself and your space, but here are a few ideas:

- **Smoke cleansing:** You can cleanse yourself and your space using the smoke from incense, healing types of wood, or bundles of dried herbs like sage or lavender. Always move your smoke cleanser in a clockwise motion around yourself and around the actual room that you're in. When cleansing tools that you'll be using in a spell, allow the smoke to swirl around the object and envision it being cleansed of anything that doesn't belong to you. Visualization is always a helpful supplement.

- **Crystal cleansing:** Like all magickal tools, crystals should be cleansed prior to use; but there are certain crystals that are believed to have powerful energetic cleansing properties of their own. One of the best for clearing energy is selenite, which often comes in the form of "wands." Use a selenite wand to clear the energy, moving it in a clockwise motion around yourself, the room, and any tools being used in your spell.

- **Sound cleansing:** The frequency of sound can be great for breaking up stagnant energy and clearing it away. If you have a bell, chime, or singing bowl, now's a great time to use it! If not, you also clap your hands (yup, that easy). Move clockwise around the room, clapping your hands together loudly. When you get to the corners of the room, clap your hands several times in an upward motion, to move the energy up and out. You can also shake out your own body through movement and let out a loud yell, if possible, to release energy and cleanse yourself.

- **Mental cleansing:** You can also cleanse yourself and your space through visualization—using the power of your own mind. Relax and envision yourself channeling a bright, beautiful beam of white light that cleanses you from the inside out. Now imagine the beam of light shooting outward. Hold the tools you'll be using in the spell and visualize each piece being bathed in the light, becoming sparkly clean. Now visualize the light beaming into the whole room, filling all empty space and pouring into each corner, cleansing all that it touches. Continue this visualization until your gut tells you you're good to go.

Many people also like to feel physically clean before casting a spell as well, which is why for some, a ritual bath is a go-to pre-spell ritual. Check out the Superbath and Supershower spells in Chapter 5 if you want to go big. Otherwise, a quick shower or a hand, foot, or face wash and a fresh pair of clothes will do just fine.

STEP 3: GETTING YOUR SH*T TOGETHER

Prepping your space and cleansing are important, but there are also a few other preparations that you'll want to bring into any ritual, mainly getting crystal clear on your personal intention for a spell and also being prepared for and familiar with the steps involved. Here's what I mean:

- **Ground Yourself:** Yes, queen, it's time to get centered. If you're truly going to be mentally present and focused on creating magick and manifesting your desires through a spell, then it's important to ground and separate yourself from the constant flow of chatter, stress, and drama in your brain. Turning our phones off and making sure we won't be interrupted is one part of that equation, but the other part is more energetic. Take deep breaths and get yourself into a present, calm, and centered space. You can also perform a quick version of the grounding ritual (page 99).

- **Get Clear about Your Intention:** Your personal intention is a huge part of any spell. That's why even if you follow a spell word-for-word, it won't be nearly as potent if you don't *feel* it and *resonate* with it. Coming into any spell with a clear and focused intention of your own that works in tandem with the purpose of the spell is a must. Again, even if a spell doesn't ask you to prepare your own words, it's still advisable to do so! Focus on the details of your unique desire throughout the course of every spell—this is what makes it unique and tailored to *you*.

- **Do your homework:** Intention is a biggie, but you also have to have your other mystical ducks in a row. That means reading through the entirety of a spell before you start it and getting your goods prepared! You don't need to *memorize* a spell or ritual, of course, but make sure you've collected the ingredients you need and are aware of the steps involved. That way you won't be surprised or caught off guard by something midritual and have to break your concentration or your circle. You don't want to realize you're missing a key ingredient midspell, or interrupt your meditative flow to reference the next step during a visualization. Obviously, it's recommended and expected for you to reference the instructions throughout a spell, but also take the time to prepare your tools and familiarize yourself with the steps beforehand so you know exactly what you're in for, and are fully prepared to get into the mystical flow.

STEP 4: CASTING A CIRCLE

Now, no need to be a traditionalist, but many witches choose to "cast a circle" to designate their sacred ritual space before beginning a spell. When you cast a circle, you're creating a circle of energetic protection and specialness around yourself. It's a way to center your magick and protect you from outside influences as you enter the mystical and sensitive headspace of spell casting. This can be as simple or complicated as you wish.

- **Casting an energetic circle:** To cast an energetic circle (the simplest way to go about things), start by sitting or standing in the area where you'll conduct your ritual and facing the north (use the compass on your phone to identify this). Envision some sort of energetic force—it could be a white flame, beam of light, forcefield—and visualize it coming through your crown. Now, using either your hand or a tool (like a wand, athame, or crystal), "direct" this visualized energy in a clockwise circle around yourself. Once you've moved a full rotation and are facing north again, feel the energy of your circle around you; this is protecting you and creating a safe space for you to enter the in-between realm of energy work where you will cast your spell.

To make your circle-casting feel complete, say the following aloud:

> **I CAST A CIRCLE, ITS BOUNDS UNSEEN**
> **TO GUIDE ME INTO A WORLD BETWEEN**
> **NORTH, SOUTH, EAST, AND WEST.**
> **PROTECT MY MAGICK, RELEASE THE REST.**

Your circle exists energetically, but you may like to use something to visually represent the perimeter, too. Some people sprinkle a circle of salt around their space, which they'll sweep up postritual; others place a candle or other talisman at the point on the perimeter that faces each of the four directions, like a square. Visualization alone works well, especially as you practice getting stronger and more assured in your energy work— but feel free to cast a circle in a more tangible way as well.

- **Calling the Elements:** Some people like to make their circle even more aligned with earth's energy by specifically calling in the four elements (which is sometimes referred to as "calling the corners"). Starting with the north, call on the energy of the direction, as well as its corresponding element. Then, if you wish, call on any other deities or energies that correspond with it. Here's something along the lines of what you could say, replacing the name of the direction and element as you go:

> **I CALL UPON THE ENERGY OF THE NORTH,**
> **AND THE POWER OF EARTH.**
> **BRING FORTH YOUR ENERGY TO CAST THIS CIRCLE.**

In addition to calling upon the elements and inviting their energies into your spell zone, you may also place a talisman representing each elements' energy at the site of each direction in your circle. This is simply an extra way to connect, so it isn't necessary. Try it if you vibe with it.

- **Leaving the Circle:** If you need to leave your circle during your ritual time for some reason, you may energetically "cut" a doorway in the perimeter of the circle where you can go back and forth without disturbing it, using your hand or a ritual tool. However, if you're gone for a while, it's worth it to recast the circle. How long it will last all depends, so use your energetic senses to see if you can still "feel" the circle's presence. If it feels weak or has totally faded, start again.

STEP 5: PERFORMING YOUR SPELL

Easy enough. No explanation needed.

STEP 6: CLOSING YOUR CIRCLE

After a ritual is finished, always close your circle, as it helps to seal the energy of your spell. This essentially involves doing your circle-casting practice backward. If you called upon the elements, you may now release them by saying something along the lines of the following:

> *ENERGY OF THE NORTH, POWER OF EARTH: THANK YOU FOR YOUR PRESENCE. I RELEASE YOU.*

You'll also want to communicate gratitude to the energy you worked with during your spell, as well as to any deities you might have called forth. Always express your gratitude to the universe! You may say something like the following:

> *WITH GRATITUDE AND TRUST FOR THE UNIVERSE, I SEAL THIS SPELL AND CLOSE THIS CIRCLE. I RELEASE ALL ENERGIES THAT CAME FORTH. I AM PROTECTED, GROUNDED, AND SAFE.*

Now envision that same energetic force you summoned to cast your circle—whatever bright beam or forcefield you visualized—and imagine yourself dissolving that energy with your hand or a tool (like a wand, athame, or crystal) as you move in a counter-clockwise direction, three times. Your circle is now closed. Do whatever you feel necessary to ground, center, and cleanse yourself postritual, and take your time integrating back into the hustle 'n bustle of regular life.

THINK ON YOUR WITCHY TOES

Improvisation is your friend! Perfection is the enemy of creativity—and it's also the enemy of an effective witchy practice. Forget about perfect. The number one most important force in your spells is your intention. Everything else is secondary and often expendable.

WITCH TIP: DON'T SPELL AND TELL

Keeping your spells to yourself until they come true can help keep your intention pure, focused, and unadulterated—and it allows you to control the narrative. While it can be fun to talk about your spells, resist the urge. Once it's over and you know the spell is complete, post it up all over town—but until then, relish this special little secret you have with the universe; it's your own private agreement and ceremony.

For this reason, don't skip a spell or ritual you feel called to just because you're missing one of the ingredients. Get creative! Swap out one herb for another one that has similar or otherwise helpful qualities. Use fresh lavender instead of lavender oil, or use patchouli oil instead of incense. Use a pink tourmaline instead of a rose quartz crystal. Use a freaking birthday candle if that's all you've got.

It's also helpful to use your own personal symbolism in rituals—in fact, I highly encourage you to do so. Add in tools that are meaningful to you, or tweak the words of a spell to better suit your desire. These tweaks will make your spells and rituals so much more powerful!

The bottom line is spells are not one-size-fits-all. Sure, there are powerful tools and ingredients that add important energy to your spells and rituals, but it's rare that a spell will lose all of its effectiveness once modified. My approach? Use what you have, and remember that *the most powerful tool in any spell is you.* Yes, you. Your intention. Your focus. Your energy. Your words. Your mind. Your magick. The rest is just extra. Your tools can enhance your spell, but without your intention and ritual, they're literally just objects.

HOW TO NOT BURN YOUR HOUSE DOWN, AND OTHER WITCHY SAFETY TIPS

Our adventures in the mystical arts could easily spiral into darkness if we were to throw all caution to the wind, which is why something that has to be brought to *every* spell is consciousness and safety. We're workin' with all kinds of stuff—fire, potent essential oils, and hello, *energy*—that has the potential to be dangerous if used incorrectly. So no matter what type of ritual you're performing, be a smart and responsible witch and take the necessary safety precautions at *all* times. It's never worth risking your safety or anyone else's. After all, you've got to be alive and well in order to enjoy the results of your spell. Duh.

Don't go up in flames: Oooh, babe, fire safety is a big one. Fire is a very powerful tool, and we work with it often in the form of candle magick, or the burning of sacred herbs or woods for smoke. Many of the spells in this book include candle work and/or smoke cleansing, so it's important that you take all necessary safety precautions.

- Never leave a flame unattended. If you're burning a candle, make sure it's on a stable surface and secured in its candle holder, and in a place where it can burn safely.

- Be very careful about using any flammable oils or alcohols if you're also working with a flame (because anything with alcohol is flammable, sweeties).

- If you're burning a bundle of herbs, do so over a firesafe dish so that you don't drop any embers. If you're burning paper or herbs, you'll also want to do this in a fireproof bowl or cauldron, with nothing around that could catch fire.

- Some candle rituals ask you to allow the candle to burn down in full. Only do this if your schedule permits and allows you to do it with safety and supervision. Otherwise, put out the candle and reset your intention upon relighting it. Do this until it's fully melted away.

Safety is essential: Essential oils are mighty powerful tools in witchcraft. However, these plant oils are *really* f*cking powerful—some are so potent and intense that they can burn your skin! When working with these oils, look up the safety measures of each before using. Some aren't meant to be used on skin, while others can be if they're diluted using a carrier oil. If you are using oils topically, do a skin test to be sure you won't have a bad reaction. Never ingest essential oils or get them anywhere near your eyes. Some oils can really hurt your sensitive eye, nose, mouth, or digestive tract membranes.

Spiritual safety is no joke, either. As a witch, you're going to get more and more sensitive to energy—and that could make you open to negative or unwanted energies, too. Yuck, *no bueno*. Practice regular cleansing, grounding, and protection techniques to keep your aura safe and clear. For spiritual safety maintenance, try the protection ritual on page 95, the grounding ritual on page 99, the cleansing bath on page 82, or make some spiritual bug spray to cleanse your space, as instructed on page 183.

Get crystal clear on crystal uses: Most crystals are totally chill to work with if you're just holding them for a meditation or admiring their sparkliness, but if you want to add crystals to your bath water or infuse your drinking water with their energy, then you'll need to do some research. Some crystals will actually break down if they're exposed to water and moisture, while others can leech out toxic chemicals into water (which would be a huge no-no for crystal water or a crystal bath). Do your due diligence and read about any crystal you plan to use for anything water-related to be sure it's safe to do.

Herbal awareness: To some, herbs are just plants—but plants are medicine, and some can actually be *really* powerful and have serious side effects. If you're using herbs in a tea, infusion, or ingesting them in any other way, research them beforehand to be sure they're safe for consumption, and okay to be prepared in the way you plan on. It's also important to source high-quality herbs. You don't want to use low-grade, pesticide-ridden plants or petals, especially if you'll be ingesting them, steeping them in tea, or soaking your body in a bath with them. Keep this in mind when foraging for your own herbs or flowers as well.

CHAPTER 5

ALL-PURPOSE SPELLS AND RITUALS

ANYTIME SPELLS TO CLEANSE YOUR AURA, GROUND YOUR SPIRIT, AND START MAKING REAL MAGICK

Here are some basic, highly useful, and easily adaptable spells and rituals that are must-have tools in any witch's book of shadows, no matter what kind of magick you're doing or what sorts of issues you're facing.

IF YOU'VE BEEN A STUDIOUS WITCH and read this book from the beginning, then you've already seen (and maybe even performed) a few simple spells and rituals—some for consecrating and creating things like sigils or a book of shadows, and others for strengthening your intuition or getting grounded. While we'll be getting into more specific spells and rituals for things like love, money, wellness, friendships, and more in future chapters, it's definitely helpful to have a small arsenal of more general spells and rituals that can be performed for all sorts of purposes, and paired with a variation of intentions. These more general spells and rituals can also be helpful for baby witches, who might want more time to practice before they hop into highly-specific spells. And that's what this chapter is all about.

The following spells go over a few things. The first two show you how to make moon water and sun water, which are powerful magickal tools on their own, but can also be very useful to add to and enhance all sorts of other spells. The next two are variations of the same classic witchy tactic: the spiritually cleansing bath. The bath and shower option are designed to clear your energy of sludge and debris so you're feeling lighter, with a squeaky clean body *and* aura—and you can also add specific intentions to these as well. Then we've got a couple of lunar scrying rituals, which help you harness the energy of a new and full moon, and practice a little bit of divination, which can bring clarity and messages from the universe for any situation on which you need guidance. And finally, we've got some basic but much-needed spells to help ground and protect your energy.

These spells are designed to come in handy for use in a variety of situations, so keep them in your witchy back pocket.

MOON WATER SPELL

○ ☽ ☽ ☽ ☽ ☽ ● ● ● ☾ ☾ ☾ ○

MOON WATER IS SIMPLY WATER THAT'S BEEN CHARGED UNDER THE LIGHT OF THE MOON. Typically, you'll want to make moon water under a full moon, as that's the energetic high point of the lunar cycle—but you can make it any time you'd like! If you're into astrology, you can also check to see what sign the moon is in at the time that you're creating the moon water, as that can also infuse it with a particular energy or usefulness.

Many spells and rituals call for moon water, which can be used in many different ways. You may drink it or even just add a few drops to your tea to infuse it with a little magick. You can add some to a ritual bath to supercharge the experience. You can put a few drops of it on a candle or herbs, or add a few drops to a bottle of perfume or lotion. Lastly, you can set a little bit out on your altar as an offering during a spell.

GET IT TOGETHER

2 clear glass jars or containers

Fresh water

(water from a natural source like spring water or rain water is preferred, but otherwise filtered water is okay)

Clear plastic wrap

Crystals and fresh flower petals, or herbs of your choice *(optional)*

---

1 This ritual is best done in the evening, around the time the sun is setting on the night of a full moon. Begin the ritual by washing your jar out so it's sparkling clean. Then use an energetic cleansing method of choice to give it a spiritual bath, such as burning sustainably-harvested sage or another cleansing herb, waving a stick of selenite around it, or simply doing a visualization and imagine it being bathed in a white purifying light. Fill the jar with water.

2 Now's the time when you add some optional ingredients to your water—although I'll note, there's no need to add anything at all, as your water will be just as powerful when charged up solely by the moon's energy. Some people like to add fresh flower petals or herbs, while others like to charge theirs with crystals. (Be sure to thoroughly research the crystal you're using before placing it in the water, as some will break down or get damaged from the moisture, while others can even be poisonous if ingested. If you can't find trustworthy info or just want to play it safe, simply place a crystal next to your jar instead.)

3 Now place your jar of water outside, where it will be exposed to the moon's light. If you don't have a safe place outdoors to leave your water, you may place it on a windowsill indoors where it'll be hit by the light of the moon. If you'd like, place some crystals around the jar, which will also energetically infuse the water. If you'd like to cover your jar, use clear plastic wrap so that the moon's light can still shine right through.

4 As you set out the water, say some words of gratitude to the moon and thank her for sharing her energy. Infuse your moon water with the following spell:

> *THANK YOU, MISS MOON,*
> *RULER OF THE NIGHT SKY,*
> *OF THE WAVES, OF THE SEA,*
> *OF THE TEARS THAT WE CRY.*
> *SEND DOWN YOUR RADIANCE*
> *THROUGH BEAMS OF LIGHT.*
> *CHARGE THIS WATER*
> *WITH ENERGY ALL*
> *THROUGH THE NIGHT.*

5 When you wake up the next morning, it's time to complete the ritual. Bring in your moon water or take it off the window sill. Remove the plastic wrap and strain out any herbs you may have used. Then seal the water in a separate jar. If you infused it with herbs, store your jar in the refrigerator until you want to use it. Some people believe moon water should not see the sunlight, but I don't believe the presence of sunlight has a negative effect. If the water was charged under the moon all night and was brought in the next morning, you've got an effective batch.

SOLAR ELIXIR SPELL

○))))) ● ● ● ● ● ● ○

EVER WANTED TO BOTTLE UP SOME SUNSHINE? This spell shows you how to make a powerful solar elixir. The process here is pretty much exactly the same as making moon water, except you'll leave it out to charge all through the day, under the sun's rays, instead of through the night.

While moon water brings an ethereal, sensitive, and quietly mystical touch to spells (and is especially potent for any spells involving love, intimacy, emotions, feelings, and personal internal work), sun water is especially helpful for louder and more outward-facing issues. It's great for bringing energy, motivation, confidence, and vitality to a spell.

A sun elixir is also very similar to a sun tea, which involves simply placing tea bags in water and setting it outside so that the sun's rays will do the heating and steeping instead of your tea kettle. Cool, right? Placing dried or fresh herbs or flower petals in water and allowing it to charge in the sunshine is a wonderful way to enhance your sun water and accompany the sun's confidence-boosting, energizing, life-giving energy for use in everyday life or specific spells.

GET IT TOGETHER

Clear glass jar or container

Fresh water

Clear plastic wrap

Fresh or dried herbs, flower petals, or crystals *(optional)*

---

1 This ritual is best done in the morning to allow your elixir to absorb the full duration of the day's light, charging and infusing itself with the sun's energy. Begin the ritual by cleaning out your jar, cleansing it with your energetic cleansing method of choice, and filling it with natural or spring water if you have it (any ol' filtered water will do).

2 Once you've filled your nice, clean jar with water, you have the option of adding whatever additional ingredients you'd like to infuse into your sun elixir, such as herbs or crystals. I think infusing sun water with herbs and flowers works especially well, as the heat of the sun can actually steep the plants in the water like a tea so you get a beautiful change of color, smell, and taste! When choosing herbs, think about the type of spells you plan on working in the near future so you can use the herbs and flowers that will support your goal. Of course, if you want to work with what you already have at home, rummage through those cabinets, round up your herbaceous options, and search for their mystical and healing properties to help you narrow things down. (Note: If you plan to use kitchen herbs that are finely ground, keep in mind that such herbs may be too small to be filtered out through a strainer. Instead, tie them up inside a coffee filter before you steep them in water.)

3 If you choose to use crystals in your water, be sure to research them to ensure they can handle being submerged and that they're nontoxic—especially if you intend to ingest the water in any way or use it on your skin. Because the sun is about willpower, confidence, energy, and spiritedness, crystals that work well with it include clear quartz (which amplifies all energy), citrine (which is great for taking action), or carnelian (a wonderful confidence-booster). If you're not sure whether your crystal is safe to put in water or just want to err on the side of caution, place it alongside the jar instead. Rest assured that solar water is powerful and potent even without any additional enhancements, so feel free to keep it pure.

4 Now it's time to set your water out to charge under the sun. Place it safely outside in the sunshine, or if you don't have a good spot outside, leave it in a sunny window where it will still receive a lot of sunlight throughout the day. If you'd like to cover the jar, do so with clear plastic wrap (this will protect the water from any contaminants but allow the sun's rays to reach it in full). Be sure to say some words or send some thoughts of gratitude to the sun for infusing its energy into your water. Say the following spell:

I GIVE THANKS TO THE POWERFUL, LIFE-GIVING SUN FOR YOUR WARMTH AND THE LIGHT OF EACH DAY 'TIL IT'S DONE. SEND DOWN YOUR ENERGY THROUGH RAYS OF LIGHT, ENERGIZE THIS WATER FROM NOW UNTIL NIGHT.

5 Once the sun has set, complete your ritual. Wash your hands thoroughly, then take your sun elixir and strain out any herbs or flowers, and remove any crystals. Seal your jar of water and refrigerate it.

THE SUPERBATH SPELL

○ ☽ ☽ ☽ ☽ ☽ ◗ ● ◖ ☾ ☾ ☾ ○

SOMETIMES WE NEED TO CLEANSE OURSELVES WITH A NICE, hot bath to get rid of the buildup of nasty, accumulated gunk. I'm *not* just talking about the kind of bath you need after a long day of sweating in the sun. I'm talking about a bath specifically for *spiritual* cleansing.

We've already talked about the importance of cleansing as witches and energy workers; spiritual cleansing is a must to keep the channel of intuition and power clear. But if you're in need of a deep cleanse or spiritual reset, then a more formal cleansing spell can be helpful—and ritual baths are one of the best and most healing ways to do it. Spiritual or ritual baths help to cleanse us of all the energetic gunk we pick up (whether it's from other people or from our own situations), leaving our auras feeling fresh 'n crystal clear.

Think of the bath as your giant cauldron. But instead of just drinking the herbal infusion or anointing yourself with it, you literally soak your entire *body* in it. Amazing, right? Soaking in a healing, purifying bath as you set your intentions can help you connect with yourself, take in the healing vibes of whatever herbs or oils you're working with, and also set the stage for a powerful spell-casting event.

There are many different types of ritual baths, but I call this one "The Superbath," because it's an all-in-one purifying, cleansing, and healing bath that'll leave you feeling refreshed and mystically renewed. Feel free to modify the supplies and swap out different herbs, crystals, or candle colors that correspond with your intention.

WITCH TIP: PRE-RITUAL SHOWER

It may seem counterintuitive, but it's advisable to take a quick shower *before* taking a ritual bath. Spiritual baths are designed to cleanse you on an energetic level, so you should go into it already physically clean to preserve the sanctity of the experience. If you don't have time to shower first, no worries—but if you do, you might find you're better able to soak up the experience.

Any combination of the following herbs
(fresh is best, but dried works, too):
Rosemary, Rue, Bay leaf, Lavender, Sage

Pot of water

1–2 cups Epsom salt

1 white candle

Fresh white flowers *(any kind you can find)*

Black and/or white crystals or clear crystals
(just one is fine, but use more if you have them!)

Florida water

1 Before you begin, decide if you would like this to be a bath for solely purifying purposes, or if you would like to have a personal intention as well (as these baths can be a powerful time for spell work). If you do have an intention (even if it's something as simple as "I invite balance to my life"), write it down so it's clear and focused. I find that simple, mantra-like intentions work best when paired with a cleansing ritual, but follow your intuition and do *you.*

2 Begin by placing your fresh herbs (as many as you'd like to use—the more the merrier) in a large pot of water and bringing it to a boil. Once it's boiling, cover the pot with a lid and bring the heat down to medium low. Allow the herbs to simmer in the water for about 30 minutes, or until you have a nice, strongly-steeped herbal infusion (it's like a very strong tea). Let it sit for a few minutes off the heat so it's not too hot when you pour it into your bath.

3 Now it's time to draw your bath. First, arrange your freshly cleansed crystals around your bathtub (some crystals can become damaged if wet, so be sure to check on the ones you're using and place them safely away from the water if so), as well as your white candle. White or clear crystals (such as clear quartz, selenite, or apophyllite, among many others) tend to have cleansing properties and help bring clarity. Black crystals (such as black tourmaline, jet, or obsidian) help absorb or deflect negative energy, and offer some energetic protection.

4 Start filling your bath with hot water. Add each item (salts, herbs, water, and flowers) intentionally and thoughtfully, infusing each addition with your personal intentions and an awareness of the spiritual properties they share. You may even thank each ingredient for the cleansing properties they offer.

- Add in a generous amount of Epsom salts (a full cup or two), as all salts are spiritually cleansing. Soaking in Epsom salt water is also detoxifying for your body.
- Pour the herbal infusion you made into the bath water (if you like the idea of bathing with herbs, which definitely adds a witchy flair, leave them in—otherwise simply strain them out!). All of these herbs are cleansing, calming, and purifying.

- Next, shake in a bit of Florida water, which is a powerful "holy" cleansing water used frequently in spiritual work. (It's actually made of alcohol and different citrus oils, so it's antibacterial and smells really good, too.)

- Last but not least, place some of the white flowers in the bath (simply remove the stem and put in the whole bloom, or pluck off the petals). White flowers in general represent purity and truth. Leave at least one white flower outside of the water.

5 It's time to step into your bath. Clear your mind of worries and feel the healing properties of the cleansing salts, herbs, flowers, and Florida water doing their work on you. Open yourself up to the energy of each of these elements. Feel the crystals you've surrounded yourself with pulsating, sending healing and negativity-banishing energy in your direction and into the bath. When your mind is calm, light your white candle. As you do, feel free to state your personal intention aloud.

6 Grab a white flower and use it to "cleanse" yourself. Hold it to the crown of your head, slowly move it down to your third eye, then move it around your head in a clockwise motion, spiraling downward until you're circling your shoulders. Smell the flower's scent as you do this, and feel it's light, airy, fairylike energy dusting away any heaviness from your aura.

7 For the remainder of your bath, your only task is to *relax*. Enjoy yourself, sister—this is your time to let go of stress and shed all the energetic crap that's been weighing on you! If you need some help embracing a relaxed mindset, close your eyes and try to meditate, or gaze into the candle's flame as a form of divination. Feel the healing water seep into your skin and detoxify you, both physically and spiritually. If you find yourself getting carried away with unpleasant or distracting thoughts, simply hold a crystal to your chest, or smell a flower and focus on your intention to center you again.

8 When you're ready, step out of the bath—but don't dry yourself off! If possible, simply stand on a towel and allow yourself to air dry, so that you can absorb as much of your healing bath's ingredients as possible. Stand outside the tub and watch as you drain the water from your bath. Say aloud the following spell:

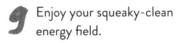

I WILL KEEP WHAT SERVES ME, BUT THE REST MAY WASH AWAY. I WILL KEEP WHAT'S MINE, BUT THE REST MAY WASH AWAY.

9 Enjoy your squeaky-clean energy field.

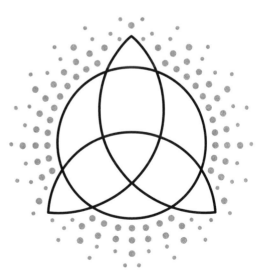

THE SUPERSHOWER SPELL

○ ☽ ☽ ☽ ☽ ◗ ● ◖ ◖ ◖◖ ○

BATHTUB-LESS WITCHES CAN STILL BENEFIT FROM THE AURA-CLEANSING AND SPIRITUALLY PURIFYING PROPERTIES that are gained from a ritual bath by setting up a healing, ritual *shower* instead. All it takes are a few modifications and substitutions, and a clear intention to purify and cleanse yourself.

This spell and ritual also comes in handy for any of you who simply prefer showers to baths. Like the Superbath, this cleansing shower offers you a powerful opportunity to set additional personal intentions and cast a spell. And feel free to modify the tools used and swap out different oils, crystals, or herbs that better support your personal intention, if you choose to set one. Otherwise, simply perform the ritual for its purifying purpose and enjoy.

GET IT TOGETHER

Small jar or container

3 tablespoons olive oil

½ cup sea salt

Florida water

Any combination of these essential oils:
Lavender, Rosemary, Peppermint, Sage

Any combination of these dried plants
(just enough to tie into a small, handheld bundle):
Eucalyptus branches, Lavender flowers,
Rosemary sprigs, Mint leaves

1 clear quartz crystal

---

1 Before you begin your ritual, decide if this shower is for mainly purifying purposes, or if you would like to have a personal intention. If you do have an intention (even if it's something as simple as "I believe in myself"), write it down so it's clear and focused. I find that simple, mantra-like intentions work best when paired with a cleansing ritual.

2 Salt is a key ingredient in most cleansing baths, as it's often used as a purifying element and also helps to literally draw toxins out of the body. Although you obviously can't soak in saltwater in your shower the way you can in a bath, you can still coat your body in its purifying benefits by whipping up a quick salt scrub beforehand. See the Witch Tip on this page for more information.

3 Gather up your dried eucalyptus branches, lavender flowers, rosemary springs, or other dried herbs, tie them together with a string, then hang them from your showerhead. Now turn on your shower and begin. Allow the water to heat up and start steaming and then enter the shower. As the hot water steams up the shower, it will release the healing scents and oils from the dried plants, which allows you to

WITCH TIP: HOMEMADE MAGICK SALT SCRUB

Showers become extra magickal when you add this homemade purifying scrub to your routine. Here's how to make it: Add ½ cup of unrefined sea salt to a small jar and mix it with 3 tablespoons of olive oil. Add a few drops of your favorite purifying or calming essential oils to the mixture (lavender and peppermint are two readily available oils with deeply relaxing and healing properties), then top it off with a few drops of purifying Florida water. Mix it all together and use it in the shower.

steam in and breathe in their healing essences. This is a great workaround for when you're unable to soak in the essences of these plants.

4 Clear your mind and allow yourself to enjoy the sensation of the warm water relaxing your muscles, washing away spiritual gunk and calming your body from head to toe. When you're ready, cleanse your body using your handmade salt scrub. This does the double duty of exfoliating and moisturizing your entire body (soft skin express!), *and* energetically cleansing your spirit using the purifying power of the salt, plus the healing power of essential

oils and Florida water. The oils will leave you smelling delightful and feeling soft postshower, too. Massage the scrub onto your entire body, starting at your feet and working your way up. As you scrub, make sure you're always pulling your scrubby strokes toward your heart. Work up to your chest from your feet, then work up each arm starting from your hands. Focus on your intention as you do this, and visualize the scrub sloughing away any negative feelings, fears, and unhappiness.

5 Now grab your clear quartz (which is okay to bring into the shower water), and use it to "cleanse" yourself. Hold it to the crown of your head, then slowly move it down to your third eye, then move it around your head in a clockwise motion, spiraling downward until you're circling your shoulders. Visualize the crystal's energy surrounding you in a cool, bright, white light of protection, frying away any darkness. Finally, hold the crystal to your heart. Say the following mantra aloud:

I WILL KEEP WHAT SERVES ME, BUT THE REST MAY WASH AWAY. I WILL KEEP WHAT'S MINE, BUT THE REST MAY WASH AWAY.

6 You may repeat it several times as you hold the crystal to your chest, if it calls to you. Visualize all the energy you've picked up from outside of you attaching itself to the water hitting your body and washing down the drain of the shower. For the remainder of your shower, your only task is to *relax*. Close your eyes and try to meditate, breathing in the scent of the herbs. Feel the calming effects of the steaming herbs and the detoxifying elements of the salt scrub healing you, both physically and spiritually. If you find yourself getting carried away with unpleasant or distracting thoughts, simply close your eyes and meditate, or hold the crystal to your chest to center yourself and refocus on your intention.

7 When you feel ready, turn off the water and step out of the shower. Allow yourself to drip dry onto a towel instead of drying off your body, as this allows the healing oils and salts leftover on your skin to remain, offering you the maximum benefits on every level. Now go off and enjoy your squeaky clean aura.

COSMIC CLARITY FULL MOON SCRYING SPELL

SOMETIMES WE NEED ADVICE, BUT WE'RE NOT SURE WHERE TO TURN FOR IT. One of the perks of being a witch is the ability to scry, to find guidance within yourself using the magick of the elements. This spell focuses on the bright point of the moon's monthly journey, the full moon, and helps you harness its cosmic energy so you can find that guidance and gain insights. Full moons are a time of *illumination*, both literally and figuratively. It's the energetic peak in the lunar cycle when the moon is at its biggest and brightest, lighting up the night sky. And if we align with the luminary's energy, we'll find that it's also a time that we're naturally able to see outside situations more clearly, or from a new light.

Take advantage of this cosmic clarity by using a full moon scrying spell to gain insight into any matter that's weighing on you. Because the full moon is a time of higher energy and illumination, it's helpful to focus on situations that involve outside elements, such as situations with work, friends, or relationships. You may not get a full play-by-play of exactly what events will unfold, but you can get some helpful clues that can guide you if you're looking for some clarity. Now stop your cryin' and get to scryin'!

GET IT TOGETHER

Dark-colored bowl or cauldron

Water

Sandalwood incense or oil

Paper and pen

1 On the night of a full moon, fill the bowl or cauldron with water and bring it to a comfortable, quiet place where you can meditate. Water represents our emotions and feelings, so don't run from them during this ritual—you'll want to embrace your emotions.

2 You may now light your sandalwood incense, or if using oil, put a drop or two on your fingertip and rub it on the back of your neck. Sandalwood is believed to offer psychic protection (which is always helpful when doing divination arts, like scrying). It's also psychically cleansing, which helps ensure you'll be seeing things clearly.

3 Close your eyes and try to clear your mind of clutter. Focus on your senses: Smell the scent of the sandalwood and feel the way your clothes rest on your skin. Pay attention to the nature of the emotions you're feeling. If you have distracting thoughts, simply acknowledge them and let them pass. Allow yourself to focus on whatever situation that you're going to be seeking guidance on through this ritual. Think through it and all you know about it. Try to dismiss the things you *assume* about it and only focus on the facts at hand. Pay attention to how these thoughts make your body feel and to any emotions they bring up.

4 Without opening your eyes, shift your focus onto visualizing the full moon that's currently outside, illuminating the sky tonight. Allow yourself to feel its energetic pull, as the waves of the ocean do. Visualize beams of the moon's glowing light shining down on you, channeling energy directly through the crown of your head. Imagine you're being charged up, like a phone plugged into the wall. Feel yourself buzzing with the lunar energy as you continue to visualize the moon's light charging you through your crown.

5 When you're ready and you feel fully "charged," open your eyes. It's just about time to scry, but before you start, speak the following spell aloud:

FROM THE GLOW IN THE SKY,
TO THE WAVES IN THE SEA,
THE LUNAR ENERGY
COMES TO ME.
IT OPENS MY EYES,
AND WITH CLARITY,
IT SHOWS ME WHAT
I NEED TO SEE.
NOW I'LL SEE WHAT I NEED
TO SEE.

6 You should now be in a more calm but energetically perceptive state. Gently blow on the surface of the water to give it a little movement, and begin staring into the bowl, past the water's surface. Let your eyes relax, almost like you're letting them go cross-eyed. Pay attention to anything you see in the water and the reflections in the surface—shapes, images, symbols, flashes of light, particular movements, *anything*—and jot things down with a pen on paper as they come to you. If any visions or images come to you through your third eye (i.e., inside your brain rather than in the bowl itself), you should write those down too, as they may be coming to you intuitively. If you feel like it, you can even pick up the bowl and hold it in your hands, closer to your face, if this makes you feel more connected.

7 Once you feel you've successfully scryed, review your notes and analyze them, looking for patterns and symbols that can offer clues as to how to move forward in the situation you were seeking guidance on. Trust that your own intuitive power and the cosmic clarity that a full moon offers have led you in the right direction.

LIGHT UP YOUR PATH NEW MOON SCRYING SPELL

○ ☽ ☽ ☽ ☽ ☽ ● ● ● ☾ ☾ ☾☾ ◖○

HERE'S A SECOND SPELL THAT HELPS US TO WORK WITH THE LUNAR CYCLE AND CHANNEL THE COSMOS FOR SOME PERSONAL GUIDANCE. Perform this spell under the new moon (also known as a "dark moon"), which marks the very beginning of a fresh lunar cycle. And it is, of course, the darkest point of the cycle, as the moon is completely shadowed and invisible. New moons are all about introspection and new beginnings. If we connect to the lunar energy during these extra-dark nights, we'll find that it's helpful for pulling our focus inward to work on our personal growth, experiences, and intuition. That said, it can be a great time to perform a divination spell on personal, private, and internal matters (in contrast to the full moon, which helps to illuminate *outside* situations).

Take advantage of the thoughtful and introspective nature of a new moon by using a flame-gazing scrying spell to gain insight into yourself and the possibility of a fresh start or new beginning. As you scry, focus on your emotions, desires, and feelings, as opposed to matters that involve other people (which is more of a full moon's business). You'll come out on the other side of this spell feeling much more self-assured about your next steps and a little more cosmically guided.

GET IT TOGETHER

1 black or white candle

Clary sage incense or oil

Paper and pen

---

1 On the night of a new moon, place a black or white candle in a candle holder. Black candles are symbolic of the dark moon and helpful for psychic protection, but white candles can be helpful for "clearing your path" and helping illuminate your visions during scrying. Light the candle and the clary sage incense. If using clary sage oil, put a drop or two on your fingertip, and rub it in the center of your forehead. Clary sage is a great oil for strengthening your intuition and "inner sight" (a.k.a. psychic vibes), making it perfect for any sort of divination. You may now light your candle.

2 Get in a comfortable position, then close your eyes and try to clear your mind of clutter. Focus on the feeling in your body and the emotions that are coming through. Try to separate the feelings from the details of your thoughts and simply acknowledge the feelings and sensations themselves. If you have distracting thoughts, that's okay— just consciously let them pass. Now allow yourself to focus on whatever personal situation it is that you're going to be seeking guidance on during this ritual. Think through it and all you know about it. Try to dismiss any anxieties or fears you have around the matter and only focus on the facts at hand.

3 Without opening your eyes, shift your focus onto visualizing the new moon in the sky—large and powerful, yet invisible—hidden by the shadows but still there. Allow yourself to feel its energetic pull, as the waves of the ocean do. Visualize the energy of the dark moon being pulled into the earth, and then visualize your body pulling that energy back up through your root chakra (which is the energy center at the base of your spine). Feel the energy moving in a circular motion—down from the dark moon, into the earth, up through your spine. Feel the dark but powerful energy charging you up, like a phone plugged into the wall. Envision the darkness of the sky like a beautiful blanket against which stars shine even brighter.

4 When you're ready and feel fully "charged," open your eyes. It's just about time for the flame-gazing, but before you start, speak the following spell aloud:

> **FROM THE DARKENED**
> **SKIES AND BLACK**
> **WAVES IN THE SEA,**
> **THE LUNAR ENERGY**
> **COMES TO ME.**
> **IT OPENS THE EYE**
> **INSIDE OF ME**
> **AND SHOWS ME WHAT**
> **I NEED TO SEE.**
> **NOW I'LL SEE WHAT**
> **I NEED TO SEE.**

5 You should now be in a more calm but energetically perceptive state. Focus your gaze on the flame of the candle in front of you. Let your eyes relax, almost like you're letting them go cross-eyed. Pay attention to anything you see in the flame, dripping wax, or smoke— shapes, images, symbols, flickers, particular movements, *anything*—and jot things down with a pen on paper as they come to you. If any visions or images come to you through your third eye (i.e., from inside your brain rather than in the flame itself), you should write those down to, as they may be coming to you intuitively. Pay attention not only to the symbolic imagery you pick up from the flame, but also to the physicality of the flame and candle itself. Is the flame calm or is it flickering? Is it large or small? Is the wax dripping evenly or to one side? Is the wick curling in any particular shape as it burns? These can all be important clues to guide your intuition.

6 Once you feel you've successfully scryed and taken what you need from the flame, read through your notes and analyze them, looking for patterns and symbols that can offer clues as to how to move forward in the situation you were seeking guidance on. Trust that your own intuitive power and the personal insight that a new moon offers has led you in the right direction.

MYSTIC SHIELD PROTECTION SPELL

ENERGETIC PROTECTION IS REALLY IMPORTANT, especially once you start feeling more comfortable doing deeper energy work. The more in touch with our own energy and intuition we become, the more likely we are to become sensitive to that of others', too. And this is a super-rad thing! It helps us feel more connected to other people and energies around us. But it also means that we're more likely to "pick things up" as we go about our day, absorbing energy that doesn't belong to us. Sometimes, dark, draining, or negative energy can attach to us and bring us down.

That said, one of the most important types of basic spells for any witch to know is a protection spell. Obviously we can't rely on spells alone to protect us from "all things scary" in the world, but it can sure come in handy if we're in a situation where we feel we need an energetic shield. That's what this mystic shield protection spell is all about.

GET IT TOGETHER

1 black chime candle

Carving tool

Sea salt

Protection oil

(use a prepared protection oil from an occult store, make one yourself, or use an essential oil of clove, rosemary, or star anise combined with a carrier oil to dilute it)

1 black tourmaline crystal *(optional but recommended)*

Smoke cleanser *(optional)*

---

1 Begin your ritual by carving a sigil of protection into your candle. You'll use a black candle, as this represents protection, and will help to ground you and strengthen your auric shield (which is the energetic force field surrounding your body that wraps you up like a nice lil' spiritual burrito). You can use any sigil you'd like. Both a cross and a pentagram are symbols of protection, if you connect with either of those; if not, you can even use a simple "X" as a symbol of protection and banishment of unwanted forces. This symbol can also be viewed as a simplified variation of the symbol of crossed spears, which is an ancient symbol of protection often used in magick.

The crossed spears represent a shield against evil or enemies. You may carve your symbol with as much detail or simplicity as you'd like.

2 Now it's time to dress your candle with oil. Rub the outside of the candle with a protective oil of your choosing. You may use a premade protection oil, or simply blend a carrier oil (like olive oil, jojoba oil, or coconut oil) with a few drops of essential oils of clove, rosemary, or star anise, which all have highly protective properties. Make sure your candle is very well "dressed" and covered in a nice, absorbent layer of oil.

3 Now spread out some sea salt (which is deeply purifying, detoxifying, and frequently used for protection in spells) on the table or work surface in front of you, and roll the candle away from you so that the salt sticks all over the oiled surface of the candle. Place the candle in a candle holder and light it, focusing on the message of protection as you do.

WITCH TIP: DIY PROTECTION OIL

It's easy to create a protective oil at home using herbs. Simply follow the instructions for the Money & Success Attraction Oil (page 132) or Goddess of Love Potion (page 111), but replace the herbal ingredients with rosemary, star anise, cloves, and sea salt, then charge it up by asking the oil to protect you instead of saying the love or money spell. Allow the herbs to infuse in the oil for a couple of weeks, shaking daily.

4 As the candle burns, it's time to do a visualization. If you're using crystals, take a freshly-cleansed black tourmaline crystal in your hands, and either stand or sit in a comfortable position. Black tourmaline is perhaps the most protective of all of our crystal friends, as it doesn't just deflect negative energy, it *absorbs* it and helps to dissipate it completely, like a crystalline filtration system, making it an even more powerful force. With this powerhouse crystal in your hands, close your eyes and allow yourself to feel comfortable and calm. Visualize all the excess energy in your body coming together to form a bright white ball of light in your core. Imagine that ball buzzing with energy—your *own* energy—and alchemizing in the light to create a pressurized inner core. Now visualize this core of energy pushing outward, moving through your body and out of your skin, surrounding your entire body like a shield of energy. Imagine it radiating out of every single pore of your body and locking into place as part of your auric field. This light isn't hot or cold, but simply bright beyond measure. Do a mental scan of your body in your mind's eye. See this bright, white energetic shield hovering outside of your body in a strong and

---

✦

WITCH TIP: QUICK PROTECTION SPELL

Doing an abridged version of this spell can be a really empowering way to start your day or counteract any negativity that you run into when you're out and about. Simply utilize the visualization portion of this ritual and repeat the spell in your head, if needed, to boost your protection quickly or on the go.

✦

---

controlled fashion, covering your head, shoulders, extremities, and core. Now visualize the bright white of the light turning into a reflective surface. Lock this into place. This is your energetic shield of protection that will disintegrate any negative energies that come near your space before they reach your physical body. The reflective surface of the shield serves as the "rubber" to outside energies, swiftly reflecting them away from you and sending them back to where they came from.

5 Once you're ready and feel comfortable and safe within your energetic shield, say the following spell aloud:

> **TO THE UNIVERSE**
> **AROUND ME**
> **AND WITHIN ME,**
> **THE ELEMENTS THAT**
> **SURROUND ME**
> **AND ARE OF ME,**
> **AND ALL FORCES OF GOOD,**
> **OF ALL BEINGS AND**
> **ALL THINGS,**
> **I ASK FOR PROTECTION,**
> **A MYSTIC SHIELD.**
> **ALL UNWELCOME ENERGIES**
> **TO MY POWER WILL YIELD.**
> **IN THE SHINE OF MY ARMOR,**
> **I WALK IN THE LIGHT.**
> **AND I CAST AWAY DARKNESS**
> **DAY OR NIGHT.**

6 Allow the spell's power to sink in, continuing to visualize the mystic shield surrounding your physical body, with trust and understanding that it will remain active and strong even after your visualization is complete. If you'd like, you may now use a smoke cleanser to "consecrate" this energetic shield over you.

7 Allow the black candle to burn down fully and safely. Your ritual is complete, and your mystic shield has been activated, protecting you from outside energies.

ROOTS OF A FLOWER GROUNDING SPELL

○ ☽ ☽ ☽ ☽ ☽ ● ● ☾ ☾ ☾ ☾ ◯

ALL OF US CAN (AND SHOULD!) actively work to ground ourselves, and get out of our scatterbrained heads to sink our awareness into the present moment and our physical body. Getting grounded is healthy for everyone, but it's an especially necessary practice when you're a witch. If you're disconnected to yourself and the elements around you, you probably won't have a strong connection to a "source," or whatever spiritual, inner self/higher power you like to call on to infuse your spells with magick. Time to slow yourself down, calm your energy, and get grounded, girl.

When grounding yourself, remember that the earth is the most useful element in this task. Anything you can use to connect with earth energy is good during a grounding ritual—plants, soil, and tangible forms of comfort (like nourishing food or physical connection) are all helpful. In this ritual, we'll be using crystals and a tangible tool to connect us with the earth element and help us ground.

Consider the seven major chakras, or the energy centers on our etheric body (meaning we can't see them, because they're made of energy). At the bottom of the column of chakras is the root chakra, which represents our foundations, security, and ability to feel safe. Think of this as the bottom of a needs pyramid. The color of the root chakra is red, so you can call on this color correspondence (along with green and/or brown) to ground you.

Use this ritual anytime you find yourself falling into an imbalanced state. If you are getting caught up in and carried away with emotions, thoughts, or passions, lean into the physical present, and "root" yourself safely back into the earth.

GET IT TOGETHER

1 brown or red candle (*optional if indoors*)

1–2 pieces of smoky quartz, hematite, or petrified wood

Cedarwood oil

---

1 You can conduct this ritual anywhere, but if you have access to a safe and quiet outdoor area, take advantage of it—this spell can be even more effective outside, where you'll have direct access to the grounding energy of nature. If you're indoors, light a brown or red candle. Either color is appropriate: Brown is the grounding color of the soil, and red represents the root chakra, which is the grounding energy force in our bodies.

2 Gather up your crystals. Some of the most effective crystals for this spell are smoky quartz (deeply grounding as well as physically protective stones); hematite (heavy crystals that are also very grounding and that help you focus your awareness in the physical and practical realm); as well as petrified wood (which is made from petrified trees or plants, and helps you "root" your energy into the earth). You may use a single crystal, but if you have two, use both, as you can hold one in each

hand during your visualization. Begin your ritual by anointing your crystals with a drop or two of cedarwood oil, which you may dilute in a carrier oil. Cedarwood oil is purifying, but also brings a steadiness of mind and body that will help ground your spirit. With the same cedarwood oil on your fingertips, rub it gently into each of your temples, and then onto the base of your spine.

3 Now sit in a comfortable position, preferably on the ground or floor (the closer you can get to the surface of the earth for this part, the better!). Close your eyes, and hold your crystal in your hands (or if using two, one in each hand). Smell the earthy, woodsy essence of the cedarwood and allow it to bring a sense of spiritual calm over your mind. Take deep breaths in slowly and rhythmically, filling your lungs with oxygen during each inhale, and then slowly releasing each exhale. Think about the fact that the oxygen you're breathing is literally produced by trees, which root themselves deep

WITCH TIP: GET YOUR FEET ON THE GROUND

If you need to ground yourself in a pinch, spend a few minutes standing or walking with bare feet on a patch of dirt or grass, and visualize your excess energy being pulled into the earth, where it'll simply become one with it. This helps you quickly connect to the natural frequency of the earth and ground.

into the earth's surface, and allow yourself to feel a part of this great and divine cycle.

4 As you enter a meditative state, try to pause any racing or intrusive thoughts by focusing your mind on your physical body. Scan yourself from head to toe, feeling the physical sensations throughout your body, such as acknowledging the sensation of the clothes touching your skin and the crystals sitting in your palms, as well as the pressure of the ground beneath your sit bones. Allow yourself to become conscious of the feeling of gravity pulling you down, down, down, ever closer to the earth.

5 Now visualize all your ungrounded energy bouncing all around you, and imagine collecting it all into a dense, supercharged ball in the core of your body—as if there's a magnet pulling it all together, reigning it in. Feel any emotional discord diffusing and any frenetic, racing thoughts subsiding. Once you've created an energy ball, visualize it shooting its energy out and down into the earth beneath you, pushing out through the parts of your body touching the ground. Pull your energy from your thoughts down into your body. Envision the energy growing cords or roots that are powerfully weaving deep into the earth, all the way down to its core. Focus also on the grounding energy of the crystals in your hands, which are helping to reign in any wild, loose energies and root them into the earth. Once you're ready, open your eyes, and say the following spell aloud:

LIKE THE TREES AND THE FLOWERS I ROOT IN THE GROUND. I AM CENTERED AND PROTECTED. DRAW MY ENERGY DOWN FROM DEEP IN THE EARTH, SHE NOURISHES ME. WE ARE ONE IN ENERGY.

6 The idea is to tap into your rootedness and groundedness. If you'd like to close your eyes once more, do so, and sit with this sensation, continuing the rooting visualization. Pay attention to the way your body picks up on or experiences physical sensations in response to this energetic shift. If you'd like, you may close your ritual by drawing the shape of a pentagram in the air in front of you, as a final grounding symbol. Move back into your day slowly and with a more deliberate sense.

CHAPTER 6

LOVE SPELLS & RITUALS

HOW TO GLOW UP YOUR LOVE LIFE & OPEN YOUR HEART TO LOVE MAGICK

Crushing, dating, sex, love, getting down, and breaking up: Love is truly a battlefield, y'all. But nothing worth working for is easy, so embrace the raw and messy nature of love by connecting with your desires through magick. Whether you're trying to be a heartbreaker or just trying not to get your heart broken, spells and rituals are a fun and powerful way to take charge of your love life.

WHAT DO YOU THINK IS THE MOST POPULAR TOPIC

for spells? If you guessed L-O-V-E, then congrats: You are correct.

And it's not hard to figure out why love spells are so sought after. Love is such a powerful part of the human experience. That's why it's *also* the #1 most popular topic at sleepovers and during late night phone calls with friends. There's no bigger thrill than the feeling of butterflies in your stomach after seeing a text from your crush, or the elated, warm-all-over sensation of a passionate kiss (or a sweet snuggle) with the person you love. Conversely, there's also no *worse* feeling than having your heart broken, feeling betrayed, or getting in a bad fight with your significant other.

Such is the wild and consuming power of love: It can take us from skipping around our bedrooms with girlish glee to ugly-crying our mascara off over a tub of ice cream in less than the time it takes to send a text message. The intense spectrum of emotion that love and romance can pull from us can feel like an out-of-body experience sometimes, and that's one reason people turn to witchcraft to make sense of it all. Because, well, love is complicated! But it's beautiful! And everyone wants to be loved! And f*ck it, we're all a bunch of romantics!

NEWS FLASH: LOVE SPELLS ARE ACTUALLY ABOUT *YOU*

Love is indeed complicated—and love spells can be, too. This is because our first inclination in a love spell is often to involve another person. Aaaaand, sorry to be a buzzkill, but that's a problem. This applies to things like trying to attract your crush, getting your ex back, making your partner fall deeper in love with you, or *anything* else that revolves around making another individual feel, think, or do something. But, per our witchy code of ethics, **it is not advisable to do spells that involve trying to control another person's feelings or actions.** This isn't to say that no good witch ever does a spell that involves another person, but if you're new to the business, it helps to leave that element out of things. Plus, as an added bonus, putting yourself at the core of your love spells is also a more effective way to tap into your own inner power and "know thyself" on a deeper level, which will make your magick even stronger. But we'll get to that.

If we center our own needs and desires on a spell rather than on our crush, lover, ex, etc., then love spells will require us to do some soul-searching to help us boil down our feelings and find the *true* intention that lies at the core of our desire for a specific person. So if you find that there's an individual at the center of your intention for a love spell, then it's time to revise your approach and start doing some research into the pages of your own lil' heart.

THREE REASONS TO LEAVE YOUR BELOVED OUT OF YOUR SPELL

1 First, de-centering any individual person in your love spells forces you to get *real* with your desires, which (as mentioned) will inherently make your spell *stronger*. The true desire at the core of a love spell is almost never *really* our actual crush or ex or partner. There's usually another deeper need or desire beneath the surface, which could be attention, moral support, validation, social status, hot sex, companionship, emotional safety, you name it—and it's way too easy to accidentally project these needs onto the person we're having feelings for. We do it all the time! Our mind is our most powerful tool, and sometimes it can craft a convincing story that makes us think an individual person will fill the hole in our heart or solve a problem that we have—when really, we can't rely on others to do that. If we do, we'll never find true, sustained happiness. We must fill those holes and solve those problems on our *own* first.

2 And that leads to the second reason why it's helpful to leave specific peeps out of your love spells. Because let's be honest—unless you know your crush on a *really* deep level, you're probably more in love with the *idea* of them than with the person themself. Practice trusting that the universe knows what's best for us, and understanding that it will bring us what we need once we state our intentions. That won't always look like what we thought initially. We can't control other people (nor should we try to), but we *can* identify our personal needs and desires. So put those out there, and accept that the universe will help connect you with someone who will meet ya there, even if it turns out not to be the person you had in mind. It'll save you stress and heartache in the end anyway!

3 The third purpose of leaving that person out of the love spell is more about *karma*. Like, hello witches, do you really want to summon up magick and energy to try to control the free will of another person? In case you missed it, karma can be a b*tch—so it's not advisable to tempt fate by trying to use your personal magick in this manipulative and frankly uncool way. Even if your spell worked, would you be satisfied knowing someone fell for you because they were bewitched by a spell, and *not* because of who you are as individuals? Imagine this scenario: Your crush falls "magically" in love with you, you quickly realize that you're not actually that compatible after all (you *know* this has happened to you) and your attraction wanes . . . but then you can't get rid of them and have to break their heart because they're totally obsessed with you *even though they really shouldn't be*. Sounds pretty off-balanced and nonsensical, right? Well, that's because there *is* an imbalance there. By trying to control the feelings, thoughts, and actions of someone else (instead of focusing on the core of your intention), you're throwing off the natural balance of the universe. You wouldn't want anyone to take your free will away, so don't try to do that to someone else—no matter how tempting it gets.

LOVE YOURSELF FIRST, B*TCH: KNOW YOUR TRUE DESIRES

If you find that all your love intentions center around a person, here are some questions to ask yourself that'll help take your crush, lover, ex, etc., out of the equation and get down to the nitty-gritty of your *actual* intentions in love:

- Why do I want what I want from this person?
- What qualities does this person have that I'm attracted to?
- What makes this person seem special or right for me?
- How would my life be better if I had the relationship I want with this person?
- What would being with this person offer me? Could I get any of these things from another source?

The answers to these questions should start leading you in the right direction. What words are coming up for you? What are the qualities, feelings, experiences you're seeking? This is probably the core of your love intention.

Maybe you've projected your need to be accepted by others onto your partner. Or perhaps you've idealized a crush out of loneliness and a desire for someone to hang out with. In either case, the desire is actually *not* the person—it's deeper than that. So don't worry if your love intentions need regular fine-tuning before beginning the magick process. This is how you start with a love spell.

YOUR MOST SIGNIFICANT OTHER IS YOU

Now that you've taken other people out of your spell and boiled it down to your true intention, you'll see that at the core of every love spell is...*you.* Your desires. Your needs. Your power.

While we can certainly *hope* that a certain someone will be the one to swoop in and meet those needs, Prince or Princess Charming-style, we simply can't guarantee that or control it. What we *can* control is how much we love ourselves—and how much that deservingness-of-love shines out to the right people in the rest of the world.

Remember the ripple effect of magic? That applies here. When you start learning to love yourself and believe that you're worthy of the love, honesty, devotion, flexibility, and vulnerability that you desire, that positive energy causes a ripple of change. Not everyone will be sensitive enough to feel the vibration, but some people will be—and those will be the people that matter.

SENSUAL HEALING: THINK LIKE A LOVE GODDESS

So much of love and romance is *sensory:* We appreciate the sight of beauty, we long for that pleasure-filled physical touch, we hear songs that send us straight into heart-flutter/shatter mode, and we're *all* guilty of having snuggled up with and sniffed a lover's t-shirt while they were away, just to take in their smell. That said, it's helpful to get in a more "sensual" mindset when trying to attract healing, change, and energy around love in our lives.

Of course, we can't do that without acknowledging and channeling the power of Venus (a.k.a. Aphrodite), the goddess of love, romance, luxury, and beauty.

Ooh la la. Venus is all about indulgence, opulence, dancin' and romancin', and of course *pleasure*—the pleasure of love, luxury, and life in general. Making like Venus and opening yourself up to pleasure, indulging in anything that feels good, and feeling comfortable in your own body is a big part of relaxing your mind and opening it up to love as well. So often, we can block ourselves from receiving pleasure. If we get too caught up in our heads, worrying about what we look like or second-guessing the things we say or analyzing a "like" or a text *way* too hard, then we miss out on the moment. We also drown out our body's natural cues that tell us how we feel about someone—and how they make *us* feel.

WITCH TIP: MOONSTONE MAGIC

Moonstones are great crystals for making us feel extra sexy. Wear moonstone jewelry when you're trying to channel your inner sex kitten; place one under your bed to up the mood if you're having someone over for some sexy time; or stick a single moonstone in your bra so it's intimately with you all day long, imbuing you with sexual confidence.

If you're planning on working some love spells, start channeling Miss Aphrodite herself by paying extra attention to your senses, specifically in regards to pleasure. Do a "pleasure scan" or even just a "sensory scan" on a regular basis as you go about your day. Notice the pleasant feeling of warmth on your skin as the sun shines through your window; take extra pleasure in savoring each bite of those French fries (*hmmm*); or literally, actually, stop to smell flowers as you pass them on the street. Wear clothes made of soft fabrics that feel luxurious against your skin. The more you realize your body is an incredible vessel that allows you to experience *pleasure*, the more open and aware you'll be when it comes to allowing someone *else* to make you feel pleasure—emotionally, physically, sexually, and otherwise. And of course, the more you love yourself and see yourself as *deserving* of pleasure, the more love you'll attract into your life.

THE LOOK OF LOVE: SYMBOLS FOR ROMANCE MAGICK

Symbolism is huge when it comes to performing spells and rituals, and there are certainly lots of universal symbols for love—many of which you'll come across in the spells to come! If you're looking to work love-related magick into your current practice, incorporate these symbols into your altar decor, your home, and your everyday life to help attract love energy:

✦

WITCH TIP: SECRET SIGILS

Use sexy secret sigils to up your love magick energy. Use a fabric marker, puff paint, or even a Sharpie to write a love sigil (either one you've created yourself or one you find elsewhere) on a pair of your underwear for a sexy, fun secret between you and yourself. As you go about your day, you'll know that you've got a lil' piece of love magick secretly being worn on your most intimate parts. This infuses your presence with attractiveness and mystery, which will make you ultra-alluring to others.

✦

- **Flowers.** Flowers are perhaps *the* iconic love symbol—is there anything more romantic than being given a bouquet? Think of the way a red rose can speak volumes. This is why roses and other fragrant flowers are often used in love spells, too. Roses in particular can be enormously powerful elements of spells. You can use fresh roses, dried rose petals, or even rose oil or incense. All will bring forth its gentle, sensual, and deeply loving energy. Some other flowers and oils that are powerful in attracting love are jasmine, hibiscus, and ylang ylang, among others.

- **The colors red and pink.** These aren't the stereotypical Valentine's Day colors for nothing. Red represents passion and sexiness, while pink represents sweet love and gentle romance. That's why both red and pink candles are popular choices in love spells of all sorts. Red and pink crystals are often used in this realm as well—ruby, garnet, rose quartz, rhodonite, rhodochrosite, and pink opal are just a few crystals that are highly effective at attracting love, healing your heart, and boosting passion.

- **The heart.** Um, this one is *obvious*. Hearts are a universal symbol of love, so doodle 'em everywhere you can to up your love energy. (You can also use a heart as a sigil and carve it into a candle in a love spell). Your *literal* heart is an important symbol in love spells too, thanks to the placement of the heart chakra, a.k.a. the energetic love and compassion center on your auric body. If you meditate, focus energy on your heart area, visualizing it glowing in green or pink, in order to help heal heartache, foster compassion for yourself and others, or otherwise open your heart to radical love.

- **Your own personal symbols of love.** It's important to think about what types of objects, images, smells, tastes, words, sounds, and experiences make *you* think of love, sex, romance, sensuality, and heart healing. If you're trying to manifest love, it's important to surround yourself with the objects and symbolic sensations that make you feel sensual, lovable, and open to being vulnerable. That can look different for everyone! Wear clothes that make you feel confident and sexy, listen to music that makes you daydream about falling in love, put on perfumes with romantic and intoxicating scents—whatever makes you feel the L-O-V-E in the air, embrace it. And incorporate this stuff into your love spells, too, as it'll bring them even more potency and personal magick.

WITCH TIP: THANK GODDESS IT'S FRIDAY

You can do a love spell at *any* time, but the best day of the week to do one is on a Friday. Friday is ruled by Venus, goddess of love, so it can be an especially good day for evoking love energy and setting intentions related to love, romance, or beauty. Plus, doing a Friday love spell puts some fresh love-spell energy on your side as you enter the weekend.

GODDESS OF LOVE POTION-MAKING RITUAL

LOVE-RELATED ATTRACTION OILS ARE PROBABLY ONE OF THE MOST POPULAR TOOLS IN WITCHCRAFT—and while it's easy to go out and buy one, it's even *more* effective to make one yourself, as it'll be fully imbued with your energy and charged up with a spell from your lips. Having an all-purpose love oil really enhances love, sex, and romance rituals, but there are so many ways to use it casually to bring some mystical love energy into your daily routine. Use your oil to anoint candles or crystals during love spells, add a drop or two to your body lotion or liquid beauty products to up your beauty magick game, throw a few drops in the washing machine while you wash your sheets to infuse your bed with mystic love vibes, throw some into a relaxing candle-lit bath, and even just put a drop or two on your wrists, temples, or chest area any time you're looking to feel more lovable and sensual.

WITCH TIP: ESSENTIAL OILS

If you would rather skip the two-week oil infusion period and use your potion immediately, opt for essential oils (highly concentrated plant oils) instead of herbs. If you do use essential oils, add about 5 drops of each oil to the carrier oil, then seal and shake. Make sure you do a skin test before using the oil to be certain you won't have a bad reaction.

The heart and soul of this love oil are, of course, the plant ingredients, which infuse it with both its heavenly scent *and* mystical powers. Rose is perhaps the quintessential love spell ingredient (and symbol of love in general), as it enhances love, attractiveness, and luck in romance, and is associated with Venus/Aphrodite, the goddess of love and pleasure of all sorts. The delicious power of vanilla is known to be an aphrodisiac, helping to relax our bodies and open us up to accepting physical affection and pleasure. And finally, there is jasmine, which brings a gentle sensuality and attracts love on a deep, dreamy, and spiritual level.

4-ounce glass jar

Glass jar or bottle

Rose (*dried petals or oil*)

Jasmine (*dried flowers or oil*)

Vanilla (*dried beans or oil*)

1 rose quartz crystal

Carrier oil

(*jojoba and rosehip oil are both good for this love potion*)

Pink, red, or silver glitter (*optional*)

---

1 You have two options when it comes to creating this love oil: You can use dried herbs or essential oils. If you use herbs, you'll need to wait a couple weeks before your oil will be ready for use, while using essential oils allows you to use it immediately. Use what you have, as either will result in a potent 'n powerful blend!

2 In a 4-ounce glass jar, add 1 tablespoon of dried rose petals, 1 tablespoon of dried jasmine flowers, and roughly 1 tablespoon's worth of vanilla beans. You may also add in a piece of rose quartz, which is the ultimate stone for love, romance, and all matters of the heart. Pour the carrier oil over the herbs and the crystal, making sure to coat and cover the herbs completely. Seal the

jar, and put it in a cool, dry place for two weeks, making sure to give the jar a lil' shake every day to ensure the herbs remain properly coated (otherwise they could start growing mold). After two weeks, you'll have a heavenly scented and highly effective herb and crystal-infused oil.

3 Now it's time to make the potion! In a jar or a cute glass bottle, pour in your infused oil. You may want to strain out the herbs to maximize the amount of oil that fits in the jar, but I often like to leave a few rose petals behind to continue infusing. If your chunk of rose quartz is small enough to fit in the glass jar, I recommend keeping it in there for added heart-opening benefits. As a final and optional step, for all you glam 'n glitzy witches out there, feel free to add some pink, red, or silver glitter to your potion. A little sparkle can sometimes go a long way in making something feel mystical, and it can give an extra "oomph" of energy to your blend.

4 Now it's time to consecrate your oil with a spell. Hold the sealed bottle or jar in your fist, then draw a large heart in the air in front of you with that same hand. Then hold the bottle to your heart and say the following spell aloud:

5 Now shake up your bottle three times. Place a drop of oil on your finger and anoint yourself behind the ears and over your heart. Use the potion however you wish, and feel free to repeat the spell upon use every time you feel your energy around love needs recharging or astral assistance.

> **WITH EVERY DROP OF
> THIS POTION HERE,
> I ATTRACT A LOVE THAT'S
> SWEET AND DEAR.
> RED LIKE BLOOD,
> HOT LIKE FIRE,
> I ATTRACT A LOVE OF
> MY HEART'S DESIRE.**

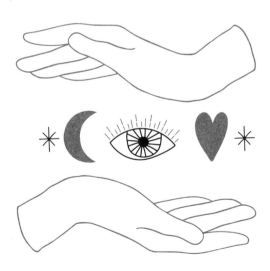

DATE NIGHT SPARKLE SPELL FOR CONFIDENCE

○ ☽ ☽ ☽ ☽ ● ● ☾ ☾ ☾ ☾ ◯

MAYBE IT'S AN OFFICIAL AND WELL-LABELLED DATE, or maybe you're just *casually* going to be running into your crush tonight. Whatever the case may be, when you know you're going to be meeting up with someone special and hoping to make a good impression, you want to go into the situation feeling *sparkly.*

On a first date, you've got two missions: Bring your authentic, confident self to the table, and assess whether you are enjoying spending time with the person you're with. This crystal ritual and confidence spell will help sharpen these skills and ensure you go into this date night or social gathering ready to crush that crush. You can do it any time before you head out, but I like to leave extra time to perform it after I've already gotten dressed and done my makeup, as a mystical finishing touch.

GET IT TOGETHER

Rose- or jasmine-scented incense

Pen and paper

1 rose quartz or clear quartz crystal

Pinch of glitter

---

1 Create a quiet, peaceful space in your zone and light up your incense (rose and jasmine are both super-sexy scents that boost our attractiveness—but any sensual, floral incense will also do the trick). Sit down and clear your mind of everything else, and make sure you're not rushed, as you want to be able to chill and focus here. Think about the qualities in yourself that make you beautiful, special, fun, and unique. (If you're not feeling great and having trouble thinking of things, try imagining what your best friend or someone else who knows you well and loves you would say!)

2 Once you've come up with some ideas, grab a pen and paper, and write down some "I" statements based on these thoughts. Your qualities could be anything, but here are some examples of how to form your statements: "I have a vast and impressive knowledge of movies. I have really nice legs. I'm really good at winged eyeliner." Write down whatever it is you love about yourself and acknowledge as a quality that makes you stand out in some small way (no matter how insignificant it may seem).

3 Now, add a final statement to your list: "I am everything I need to be and more." Because it's true—whether or not you believe it yet.

4 Take your quartz crystal in your hand and hold it as you now speak your "I" statements aloud in front of a mirror. You are charging your crystal with the power of these intentions. This might feel *really* awkward at first, but the key is to repeat them until it feels *not* awkward. Own it. Say them each ten times if you need to. These are *your* qualities and *your* truths. It's okay to celebrate these things about yourself—especially because these are some of the things you'll want to show off as you're out making an impression on someone new and showcasing the brilliant and unique individual that you are! You want to bring your most authentic and proud self into whatever situation you're going into tonight. You are *enough*, and there's nothing and no one you need to be but yourself.

5 Hopefully, now you're feeling a little more confident and focused on your most sparkly qualities, so now it's time to put some things into perspective by sharpening your energetic vision. It's easy to get really caught up in focusing on ourselves and making a good impression on a first date. But remember, the impression *you* make is only half the equation. The other person is also auditioning for *you*, sweetie—so stop worrying so much and focus some energy on being able to slow down and see that, too. This person isn't granted an automatic second date, even if they *are* absurdly hot.

6 Now hold your quartz crystal to your forehead, to energetically clear your third eye (or your spiritual eye). This is to help you see things clearly on your date and keep everything in perspective. As you do so, remind yourself that all you have to do is be *you*, and pay attention to how this person makes you feel.

7 Finally, it's time to enact the spell. Sprinkle a small amount of glitter into your palm and close your fist. Speak the following spell aloud three times. As you do so, envision your words being imprinted into the glitter's sparkly energy:

MY BEAUTIFUL FACE WILL
SPEAK THE TRUTH.
MY BEAUTIFUL EYES
WILL SEE IT, TOO.
MY MIND WILL SPARKLE,
MY SOUL WILL SHINE.
THE LOVE I DESIRE
CAN BE MINE.

8 As you say this a third and final time, sprinkle the glitter over yourself (keep it super minimal— unless, of course, you're going for a disco ball vibe). If you have some glitter leftover after adding a touch of sparkle to your hair or outfit, you can sprinkle it onto your altar or into

a candle. If you really hate the idea of having some glitter on you for your outing (as a glitter lover, I don't get it, but I respect it), then you can put it into a small satchel to keep in your purse, or paint some onto your nails with a coat of clear polish. If someone asks where all the glitter came from, there's no need to give away the fact that you did a witchy spell before your date; just say you like to sparkle. Throw your charged-up quartz in your purse with you to bring the confidence-boosting energy of your words with you all through the night.

SPICE UP YOUR LOVE LIFE SPELL

○)))))) ● ● (((((○

EVERYONE GOES THROUGH A DRY SPELL FROM TIME TO TIME. If there hasn't been much action on the love life front lately, it's time to inject a little firepower and energy into your game. Cinnamon brings heat and spiciness to any situation, while the energy of fire represents burning desire and passion. Ooooh-la-la. Let's end this dry spell and spice things the f*ck up. If you're ready for this period of romantic solitude to end and some fun affairs to begin, then it's time to spice up your life—your love life, that is—with this fun and spicy spell.

GET IT TOGETHER

1 white chime candle

1 red chime candle

Warm tea, red wine, or apple juice

Cinnamon

Sugar or agave syrup

A favorite bad-b*tch song to dance to

---

1 Let's get spicy. Begin your ritual by preparing and lighting two candles: One white, and one red. First, we're incorporating candles here specifically for their *heat*. We're trying to make your love life hot, hot, hot, so the fire energy is exactly the element we want to work with. The white candle represents cleansing

energy to help clear any blockages from your path, and the red candle represents sultriness, passion, and romantic intensity—all of which you're inviting in.

2 Now that your candles are lit, you're going to make your sweet and spicy love elixir! Heat up a cup of tea (whatever kind you like is fine, but preferably something stimulating rather than something sleepy). If you don't want to use tea, you may use a small glass of red wine instead. Add approximately half a teaspoon (or a healthy pinch) of cinnamon into your glass, and say aloud, "to add some spice." Envision the steamy, sexy, passionate way that you want to feel in love. Then, add some sugar or agave syrup to taste, and say aloud, "to add some sweetness." As you do, think of the type of sweet, gentle, romantic moments you want to experience as well. Envision these experiences swirling into your future reality.

3 Stir the mixture *clockwise* with a spoon. As you stir slowly and intentionally, in a clockwise motion, say the following spell aloud:

THE HEAT OF DESIRE,
THE SPICE OF LOVE,
THE WARMTH AND ZEAL
OF THE SUN ABOVE,
THE THRILL OF PASSION,
MAY CATCH MY EYE
LIKE THE MYSTIC ALLURE
OF THE MOON-LIT SKY.
QUENCH THE EARTH'S THIRST
LIKE A SUMMER RAIN,
NOURISH THE SEEDS OF
MY PASSION AGAIN.

4 Stir the tea until the cinnamon and sweetener are blended (it's okay if the cinnamon remains a little clumpy—that's normal!) and it's cool enough to drink. Slowly sip your elixir, noticing the warm, comforting temperature of the liquid as well as the sweet and spicy flavors that have blended with your tea or wine. Focus on the personal intention that you created going into this spell, and take this moment to really visualize the feelings, sensations, tastes, sounds, and sights you hope to bring into your romantic life. Envision this new reality pouring into you and becoming part of you.

5 Now let's get even more physical. Turn on the song of your choosing. This should be a true bad b*tch *anthem* that makes you feel sultry and *sexy*. Turn on *that* song. And now... dance. Get into it. Move slowly and sensually. Shake off any self-conscious feelings that come up—no one's watching, so no need to hold back! Up the tempo if you'd like. Pretend you're a video girl. Let *loose*. If you haven't yet finished your elixir, you can continue drinking it as you move. Dance at least until the song is through (although you're free to continue!). Allow your candles to burn down safely. Your spell is complete.

'SHIP IT LOVE SPELL JAR

○ ☽ ☽ ☽ ☽ ● ● ☾ ☾ ☾☾ ☾○

BEING SINGLE IS COOL—we are independent witches and we definitely don't need a partner to complete us. But if you're ready to go balls-to-the-wall into a "relationship" then this spell can help you attract someone who's in it to win it—and *ship* it. Because playing the field is fun, but when we're ready for commitment, we're looking for something a little deeper.

Creating a spell jar is a great way to, quite literally, bottle up your intentions and create a symbolic object that can help propel your desires into the ether. Remember, this spell isn't about attracting a specific individual (even if you've got your heart set on someone). Trust that the universe knows best and will answer your spell in the way it's meant to be.

GET IT TOGETHER

8½ x 11 sheet of paper, a bunch
of small squares of paper, and a pen

Small glass jar or corked craft bottle

Dried orange peels

Dried rose buds

1 small rose quartz crystal

Patchouli oil or perfume
(or another love oil of your choosing)

Vanilla oil or extract

Dried dill or lavender *(optional)*

Sugar

Glitter *(optional)*

1 red candle

---

1 Begin this ritual by thinking of all the qualities you're looking for in a partner and writing them down in a list on the sheet of paper. It's okay to get specific and even a little picky! Now is *not* the time to lower your standards. If you have a current love interest, remember—this spell is NOT about them. If there is a person you have in mind, refer to the instructions at the beginning of this chapter. Think about what you love about this person and how you would feel if they wanted you, and let their qualities guide you. The universe can help orchestrate a relationship that's right for you, but in order for it to do so, you have to trust that it knows what it's doing. Tell it what you desire in a relationship, and it'll help to make it happen, okay?

2 Next, you're going to start filling your jar with some of its contents. Start by gently layering some dried orange peels and dried rose buds at the bottom of the jar. (Note: You can definitely dry these out yourself, if you have access to fresh roses and oranges!) The rosebuds represent a new beginning in a loving relationship, while the orange peels represent the ability to attract a sweet, exciting, and successful romance. Depending on the size of your jar or bottle, you may

need to cut the dried orange peel into small pieces, and that's okay.

3 Then you'll add at least one piece of rose quartz, which is a quintessential love stone that helps attract a compassionate, gentle, and committed type of love. You will need to find a piece of rose quartz small enough to fit inside your jar.

4 Next, draw the following sigil on the same piece of paper. This sigil symbolizes attracting a partner and a romantic relationship. (If you've already created your own sigil for attracting a lover, you can use that instead!)

As you draw the sigil, concentrate on the qualities written on your piece of paper.

5 Next, you'll want to add a few drops of patchouli oil (which is wonderful for drawing potential partners onto your path), as well as a few drops of vanilla oil or vanilla extract (which boosts your overall attractiveness and confidence). If you'd like, you can add a final touch of dried dill or lavender as a sprinkle on top. Dried dill will help to attract a masculine partner, while lavender will help to attract a feminine partner.

You may use both or neither, if you don't have a preference. You may also add some glitter or any other small items that have special meaning to you in this context. Fill the rest of the jar with sugar, which represents sweetness and adds a delightfully delicious energetic aftertaste to the rest of the spell.

6 The final step is speaking the spell and then sealing your jar or bottle. Light the red candle and focus on the flame—burning bright, hot, and passionately like the love that you're inviting into your life. Imagine the flame is the light that's attracting a lover of this quality to you (sorry to liken your future lover to a moth, but you get what I'm saying). As the flame burns, speak the following spell aloud (which includes the list of qualities you're seeking in a future partner):

+ A PASSIONATE LOVER, +
COME TO ME.
A COMMITTED PARTNER,
I'LL SOON SEE.
IN A RELATIONSHIP
+ BUT STILL FREE, +
CLOSE TO EACH OTHER,
AS WE CHOOSE TO BE.
HERE ARE THE QUALITIES
I DRAW TO ME:

(SAY ALOUD THE QUALITIES YOU SEEK IN A ROMANTIC PARTNER.)

7 When you're finished, roll up or fold up the sigil and place it inside the jar. Now it's time to seal the jar. Put on the lid or cork, and then using the hot wax from the red candle, carefully pour it over the edges of the jar or bottle and quickly seal it by either screwing on the lid or popping in the cork. Allow the red wax to dry. Keep your jar on your altar or in a sacred spot. Once your spell has come true, you may empty the jar of its contents and cleanse/reuse it for your next spell jar.

CUTEST COUPLE CANDLE SPELL

○ ☽ ☽ ☽ ☽ ☽ ● ● ● ◖ ◖ ◖◖ ◖ ◖ ○

IT SEEMS THAT EVERYWHERE WE TURN, THERE'S A TON OF FOCUS ON DATING AND FINDING LOVE. But what about those of us who *have* found love? This is a spell for all you boo'd up people. Just because we're in a committed relationship doesn't mean the work is done. Being in a relationship takes a lot of effort and comes with a whole host of potential struggles, so sometimes it can be helpful to infuse that partnership with a little bit of consensual couple's spell magic.

Doing a spell with your lover can be a really fun and unique bonding experience—and more importantly, it can help to strengthen your relationship, promote honesty and acceptance, and remind you to support each other in your individual journeys. Remember the rule that your intention should never include another person? Well, there is an exception to that rule, and that is when the person involved gives you their clear consent. This ritual involves more than permission—it also involves the active participation of your partner! So chat with them about their willingness to strengthen your bond through a love spell, and respect their wishes either way—make sure that both of you are on board! This is a spell *a deux*, so you can't do it solo.

*The purpose of this spell has nothing to do with controlling anyone's will—it won't force love to appear where it isn't anymore, or make someone stay if they don't want to. What it will do, however, is bring honesty and authenticity to your relationship. That doesn't necessarily mean staying together forever; it does mean respect, openness, and a willingness to be real about feelings and address troubles as they come for as long as you are together.

GET IT TOGETHER

2 red chime candles

1 white chime candle

Love oil *(optional)*

Carving tool

1 apple

Paring knife

1 Before you begin your spell, let's do a quick communication check: Have you and your lover read through the instructions together and both agreed this ritual resonates with each of your wills? If so, great—let's begin!

2 Using your carving tool, you should each carve your name into one of the red candles. Each of these candles represent your individual passion and ability to love yourself and one another. Then, carve a heart into the white candle (if you'd like, you can each carve one half of the heart, so it's a joint creation), as this candle symbolizes purity and honesty in your love. If you have a love oil, use this to anoint each of the three candles, rubbing the oil over the entire surface of the candle from base to tip.

3 Light the white candle, and set it in the middle of the table or surface between the two of you. Then, each of you should take the red candle with your name on it and together, in unison, hold the wicks to the flame of the white candle, igniting them both at once. As you hold your individual candles together with the white candle's flame of purification, say the following spell (either at the same time or in succession):

I COMMIT TO HONORING MYSELF. I COMMIT TO HONORING YOU. I COMMIT TO HONORING THE RELATIONSHIP WE SHARE, IN ALL ITS FORMS.

4 Now set your red candles down on either side of the white candle, allowing them to burn safely down. In front of the flames, slice a crisp, fresh apple in half, cutting it width-wise rather than vertically so it'll be separated into two halves. As you open it, you'll see that cutting it in this way exposes in the center of the apple a beautiful five-pointed star, which represents the balance and wholeness of the four basic elements and the fifth element, which is spirit. Apples in general represent fertility, truth, and desirability.

Each of you should hold one half of the apple in your right hand and say the following spell:

WITH CLARITY AND BALANCE, BELOW AND ABOVE, I OFFER YOU HONESTY, KINDNESS, AND LOVE.

5 Now each of you should bite the apple from the other's right hand as your cross arms. Take your apple back and finish it yourself. Seal the spell with a kiss, and the spell is complete!

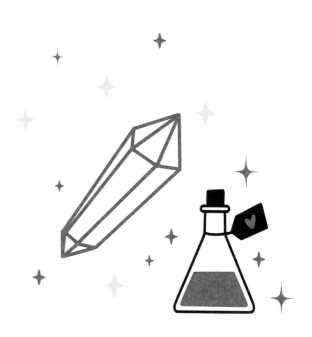

HEARTBREAK HEALING CORD-CUTTING SPELL

○ ◗ ◗ ◗ ◗ ● ◗ ● ◖ ◖ ◖ ◖ ○

ENDING A RELATIONSHIP OR REALIZING YOU WON'T GET WHAT YOU WANT FROM SOMEONE YOU LOVE does a tough number on the heart. If you're in the throes of heartache and heartbreak, it may be time for a letting-go spell, to finally release the hold that you're keeping on the idea of a person when really you should be moving on. This is a very simple but effective spell.

Remember to keep it real: Don't perform this spell until you're actually, no-bullsh*t, ready to let go of this heartbreak. If you're still holding out hope that someone will suddenly change their mind or come back to you, then you're not ready to perform this spell. It will only be effective if you're willing to commit to moving on! The spell can't do all the work for you—it simply serves as a spiritual booster for your own commitment to independence.

GET IT TOGETHER

Pen and paper

2 small chime candles or tea lights
in jars or candle holders *(any color)*

1 piece of string, ribbon, or yarn

Scissors

Firesafe bowl or cauldron

1 white chime or 7-day candle

---

1 To begin this spell, don't think of the person you're letting go of, but rather the *feelings* that this person incites in you right now. Write down the negative feelings that have emerged through this heartbreak—all the pain, heartache, fear, and loss you've experienced.

2 Now prepare your two candles. These candles represent you and the relationship you're letting go of. Take your string and tie one end around each candle's candle holder (but don't tie the string onto the candles themselves, as the flame will eventually reach it and could present a fire hazard). When the candle holders are tied together, light both of the candles. Repeat the following spell three times, and upon finishing the third chant, cut the string holding the candle holders together.

3 Congrats, babe: You have officially cut spiritual ties with this relationship. You should allow your candles to burn safely, but before they go out, take the piece of paper with all your pain written on it and set it on fire with the flame of one of the candles. Immediately place it into your cauldron or firesafe bowl to burn into ash.

4 Take the bowl full of ashes and bury the ash somewhere outside in the soil. Burying the ashes of this relationship in the earth allows it to grow into something new. This experience doesn't just disappear— you're always shaped by the memory of it—but it can be fertile ground on which your future can grow. Burying it represents that. Light a white candle after the spell to help clear your path for new beginnings.

**TWO USED TO BURN AS ONE,
BUT NOW THAT
PHASE IS DONE.
NOW ONE BURNS AS TWO.
I AM ME, AND YOU ARE YOU.**

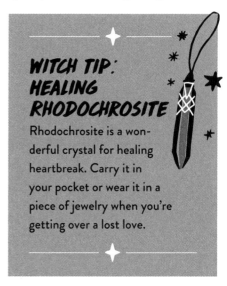

**WITCH TIP:
HEALING
RHODOCHROSITE**

Rhodochrosite is a wonderful crystal for healing heartbreak. Carry it in your pocket or wear it in a piece of jewelry when you're getting over a lost love.

CHAPTER 7

ABUNDANCE SPELLS & RITUALS

HOW TO BE A BOSS-ASS WITCH INSTEAD OF A BROKE-ASS B*TCH

Whether you're looking to do a spell to increase your abundance, bring some quick money your way, get a job or promotion, or just sprinkle some good luck over your personal finance department, there's a spell you can perform to help you achieve it.

OKAY, LET'S TALK MONEY, HONEY. We want it, we need it, and even if we sometimes *hate* it (capitalism, I tell ya!), we can recognize that it's a form of currency that we rely on to survive in this mad world we live in. We're all on our hustles— whether we're hustling up the corporate ladder, hustling for an admission into the college of our dreams, or just hustling to get to our shift at the coffee shop on time after a long night of partying with the coven. There's money to earn and fame to gain and goals to achieve, so we've got to stay on top of our game. And of course, things like your career, education, and passion projects can totally fall under this witchy umbrella, too—because these are all routes to financial freedom.

But I get it. Our society's obsession with money can admittedly be exhausting. We're bombarded by it—in songs on the radio and ads on social media, and it's hard not to notice that it's the rich and famous one percent of the population who seem to rule the world. But money isn't some elusive, impossible thing to catch. Money is simply a form of *energy*, like anything else. There are systems—or rituals, in our case—that can work to bring this money energy your way. Obviously there are a *lot* of factors that limit people's access to success (that's real—and everyone is born with a different level of financial privilege and roadblocks), but opening your mind-set up to money energy certainly doesn't hurt—in fact, for many witches, it *really* helps. **If we think of money as a form of energy, then we can start opening up channels and portals in our consciousness to let that energy flow in. Because as witches, energy is our *thing*. We can create, change, and work with energy—money is no different.**

When we talk about this kind of success, we're not just talking about a greedy need for cold, hard cash, diamond rings, and expensive-ass sneakers. We're talking about *abundance*, b*tches. Abundance is more than just money—it's the feeling of being taken care of, of having all that you need, having what you desire. Abundance is also a *trust* that the universe is going to pull through for you and provide for your needs. And I get it—we live in a cutthroat society and we trust no one. But the universe isn't just any ol' someone—you've got to believe that the universe has got your back.

Before you embark on career, money, and abundance-related spells, there are a few ways to empower your boss-ass self and get into a high-vibe, money-attracting, abundance-friendly mindset.

GLOW-UP YOUR MINDSET

A huge part of executing successful abundance rituals is entering the right mindset (but you know by now that this is true of *any* type of ritual!). When it comes to your mindset and conditioning about money, it can be a heavy load to unpack. So let's sort through the ol' financial files of your mind and heart to clear space for what you really want, witches.

ABUNDANCE SCAN

If you're looking to bring more abundance into your life, start by practicing a daily abundance scan ritual. At least once a day, scan your surroundings and look for signs of abundance. If you're in your bedroom for example, what do you see? Maybe a comfortable bed with a fluffy comforter? A stack of vinyl records of artists that you love, perhaps? A nice breezy window with a view of a tree outside? Identify anything that feels abundant to you—or that provides a sense of luxury and makes you feel *lucky*. Now ask yourself: Are you taking advantage of the abundance that's already all around you? For example, make your bed—don't let it stay messy-looking all day! Instead of letting those records collect dust, organize them and throw one on while you do your makeup in the morning! Open the shades on that breezy window with a view—even if you're only spending a few minutes in your room during the daylight today! If you're not actively aware and appreciative of the abundance that's already all around you, how can you expect to be aware and appreciative of the abundance you conjure up with your spells?

CLEAR OUT OLD SPIRITUAL BAGGAGE AROUND MONEY

Another helpful tool to developing an abundance-welcoming mindset is doing a little self-therapy to clear out any old spiritual baggage you might be carrying around regarding money. Nobody needs that sh*t. Ask yourself: What views about money and success have you inherited from your parents or guardians?

I don't know about you, but my family had some hard times with money while I was growing up, and these financial struggles instilled in me a huge fear of debt, credit cards, and spending beyond my means—which gave me a major scarcity-based mentality about abundance. For years, even if I was in a good place financially, I always feared some kind of scarcity in the future (as if what I had was about to be taken from me). Unpacking and addressing issues like this can open up pathways to a new sense of abundance and a trust that you can achieve your goals.

MONEY SYMBOLS

All spells call for a list of supplies and ingredients, including the abundance spells here. Certain objects and symbols represent abundance in the collective consciousness, and there are many herbs and crystals with specific abundance-related correspondences. Here are some that can be used in spells and rituals, displayed on your altar or in your home, and worked into your daily life to help manifest success in money, wealth, and work:

+

WITCH TIP: RESPECT THE PURSE

It's an old superstition that you should never set your purse on the floor, as it's believed to show a lack of respect for your money. And that makes sense: Things that are important to us usually have a designated place and aren't just tossed aside on the ground, right? So we should treat our purse—which holds our wallet and our money—the same way! Hang that baby on a wall hook, a door knob, or at least set it on a couch or table top. I'm messy as hell, and usually toss my sh*t into a pile on the floor of my living room as soon as I breeze through the front door—but no more, witches!

+

- **Coins, money, and precious metals.** This is perhaps the most obvious of all abundance symbols—money and precious metals themselves! If we're manifesting money, there's no better tool to work with, even if it's in small amounts. Even if a handful of coins can't buy you much, their shiny appearance and the jingle they make in your hand sure feels abundant. Display bowls of shiny dimes or golden coins in your home or on your altar. Ask for crisp, fresh bills at the bank (even if we're just talkin' single dollar bills, y'all) and smell the scent of cold, hard cash. Even just doodling dollar signs can help evoke the power of the dolla'!

- **The color green.** Green is the color of money, and it makes sense why—as green is also the color of abundance in nature itself (think of rich, rolling, grassy hills and lush, luxurious blooming green gardens). Use green candles in spells that involve attracting wealth and abundance. Green crystals (such as jade, green aventurine, peridot, moss agate, and malachite) are also helpful in attracting material wealth, bringing luck and opportunity in matters of money, and clearing blockages around issues of financial stability.

- **Pentacles.** Pentacles are literally just five-pointed stars, but they serve as a magickal symbol for the element of earth. This is the symbol that pertains to earthly matters and tangible, physical wealth. So things like work, finances, money, riches, and material luxury all fall under the realm of the pentacle. Similarly, in tarot cards, the suit of pentacles typically represents material wealth, finances, and tangible earthly matters. Display a pentacle on your altar to summon some earth energy or doodle this symbol to evoke its power.

- **Your own symbols of abundance.** It's important to think about which objects, images, smells, tastes, words, sounds, and experiences make *you* think of abundance, wealth, and success. If you're trying to manifest money and financial success, it's important to surround yourself with the objects and symbolic sensations that scream abundance to *you personally* in order to get you in the right mindset. You can also, of course, incorporate these things into your rituals to give them a personal flair.

WITCH TIP: PURIFY THAT WALLET

Clean out your messy-ass wallet, sister. If your wallet is full of crumpled receipts, ancient high school IDs, and random gift cards with twenty-five cents left on them, let your spirit be cleared of all this clutter. Your wallet holds your money and your plastic—respect it as a symbol of your prosperity and keep it clean!

MONEY & SUCCESS ATTRACTION OIL SPELL

○ ❭ ❭ ❭ ❭ ❭ ❭ ● ● ◖ ◖ ◖◖ ◖○

A MAGICKAL OIL BLEND IS A CLASSIC TOOL IN WITCHCRAFT.
It can really enhance your spells and rituals, and can also be used casually to infuse your day-to-day life with a little magick. With a money- and success-oriented oil, you can attract tons of abundance in your everyday life. Rub a drop of it on your money, wallet, or debit card to help bring financial good luck. Use it to anoint candles or dab onto crystals in abundance spells. Sprinkle a small amount on your desk at work to boost success. Put some on your third eye while doing abundance-related visualizations. Or apply a drop or two on your temples, wrists, or ankles to bring you good fortune during a job interview or any other success-related endeavor.

Some of the major power sources of this oil are, of course, its plant ingredients; they make this potion smell earthy and delish, and also infuse it with tons of herbal magick. Patchouli represents the element of earth and is one of the most potent oils for money spells, as it attracts strength and good luck in all sorts of financial endeavors. Bergamot's bright and citrusy scent is also a major money-attractor, and it brings prosperity and helps you balance your checkbook (as well as your mindset). And basil is great for business, financial growth, and stability.

GET IT TOGETHER

4-ounce glass jar or bottle
Carrier oil (both jojoba and olive oil work well)
Patchouli oil
Bergamot oil
Basil oil
1 tiny magnet or lodestone
Green or gold glitter (optional)

---

1 In a 4-ounce jar or a cute glass bottle, pour in the carrier oil, then add approximately 10 drops of each oil you'll be using. I also advise dropping a small magnet or a lodestone (which is a naturally magnetic type of rock) directly into the oil to infuse it, as magnets of any kind act as symbols of "attraction" and bonding, which can give a *magnetic* energy to any money spell and help to attract money your way. If you have any other oil-safe abundance-related amulets that you'd like to add to your oil (like a lucky penny, a clover, or gold flakes), feel free to incorporate that as well.

2 If you want to be extra fancy, add a little green or gold glitter to your potion (I personally feel a little sparkle can sometimes go a long way in making a witchy craft feel more mystical, and it can give an extra "oomph" of energy to your blend.)

3 Now it's time to consecrate your oil with a quick spell to charge it with even more power and energy. Hold the sealed jar in your hands, then use it to trace a large dollar sign in the air in front of you. Say the following spell aloud:

WITH EACH DROP OF THIS OIL, ABUNDANCE FLOWS. WITH EACH STEP, WITH EACH CHOICE, EVERYWHERE I GO I ATTRACT WEALTH AND I ATTRACT MONEY. FORTUNE COMES TO ME LIKE BEES TO HONEY.

4 Now shake your bottle three times. Place a drop of oil on your finger and anoint yourself on your third eye, as well as at the base of your spine. This connects your root chakra (which represents stability and foundations) with your third eye chakra (which represents your intuition and imagination). If you'd like, you can meditate while visualizing yourself acquiring the material wealth, lifestyle, job, or opportunity that you desire. Imagine it becoming part of your daily life. Also focus on the feeling of generosity and giving—as you will always receive more when you're willing to give. Allow this oil to rid you of a "scarcity mentality" around money and trust that there is enough for everyone.

5 Use the potion however you wish, and feel free to repeat the spell every time you feel your energy around money, finances, wealth, or abundance needs recharging or astral assistance.

TWO-BUCK LUCK SPELL

○)))))) ● ● ● ● ● ● ● ○

$2 BILLS ARE SO FUNKY, RIGHT? The world already has plenty of $1 bills around, and people rarely use $2 bills, so it seems so *random* that they're still around. However, they are and there's a superstition that if you hide a $2 bill away in your wallet, it'll ensure that you'll never be broke. I like this superstition because I never want to be broke (duh!) and honestly, $2 bills are kinda quirky. But also in numerology, *2* is a number of *balance*—and achieving balance in and bringing luck to your financial life is the goal of this spell.

GET IT TOGETHER

A $2 bill *(which you can get at any bank)*
**Bundle of sustainably-harvested sage
or other smoke-cleansing herbs**
Paper and pen
Nice inky pen or permanent marker
Patchouli incense and/or oil
Gold star stickers, glitter pen *(optional!)*

---

1 Begin this ritual by practicing an abundance check in your ritual space and then meditating on the feeling of financial freedom. Really visualize what it would feel like to have an innate *knowing* that you'll never have to worry about money, that you'll always be provided for in some way. Light your bundle of sage and slowly cleanse the $2 bill by passing it through the stream of smoke.

You should cleanse all magical tools before a ritual, but this is *especially* important when working with money, as it passes through so many hands and comes into contact with so much energy.

2 When you're ready, think about distilling the feeling of financial freedom that you felt during your visualization into a simple, one or two-sentence mantra. This is your *spell*. It should be something that feels good to say and rolls off your tongue. Write out a paragraph to get your thoughts down on paper if you need to! If you'd rather, feel free to use this simple spell:

I AM FOREVER FULL OF ABUNDANCE. THE UNIVERSE PROVIDES FOR ME. ALL THE MONEY I COME IN CONTACT WITH THE UNIVERSE RETURNS TO ME TIMES THREE.

3 Hold the bill in your hand and say the spell aloud three times, feeling the power of your words infuse your bill with energy. Now write this mantra directly onto the $2 bill using a nice, pleasant-to-write-with inky pen or marker.

4 Once your spell is written, light some patchouli incense or add a few drops of patchouli oil to a diffuser or oil burner as an offering and a thank-you to the universe (patchouli

is easy to find anywhere that sells incense or scented oils)—because showing gratitude is always helpful, especially in spells of abundance. As you did with the sage smoke, pass your (now-magical) $2 bill through the patchouli smoke (or anoint it by rubbing a drop or two of patchouli oil directly onto the bill). Envision the smoke and oil as being positive, healing, abundant energy, infusing your $2 bill with magick and turning it from a simple piece of paper into a symbolic and magickal charm.

5 Now it's time to get crafty, witches. Adorn your bill with anything that feels sparkly, magical, and abundant to you, like some shiny gold star stickers, glitter pen doodles of pentacles or dollar signs, or anything else that turns this from a simple two bucks into a supercharged talisman. Or leave it as is, adorning it only with your spell and intention (which truly is powerful enough). When the spell is complete, fold up the $2 bill and place it in your wallet, preferably in a pocket or somewhere else where it won't get lost (and you won't be tempted to spend it). Leave it there to work its magic—and to remind you of your intention each time you're rummaging for cash!

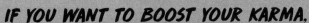

IF YOU WANT TO BOOST YOUR KARMA,
make three additional $2 spell bills and give them to friends!

GLOW IT UP & GROW IT UP CAREER GOAL MANIFESTATION SPELL

IF YOU'VE GOT CAREER GOALS, trust that there is magick afoot to help you achieve them. Our goals are sort of like seeds. They're brimming with the magick of new life and the potential to grow into a big, beautiful plant. Of course, after planting the seed in the soil, we can't simply walk away. What would happen to it if we never watered it, trimmed it, made sure it had sunlight? Well, there would be a good chance it wouldn't flourish or grow into the glorious plant it could have been. The same is true of our goals. Once we "plant" them or decide to manifest them, we must continue devoting our energy toward them to ensure they grow into the reality we want them to be.

For this ritual you'll be planting basil, which has huge power when it comes to bringing energy to career goals. If your goals are related to your current job or passion project, it's ideal to keep the basil plant you'll be planting in your workspace—whether that's in your office or your desk at home. However, if you're trying to manifest something completely new or you don't have a workspace that would work for this, you can also simply set this up on your altar or in the northern area of your home, which in feng shui is considered the career/life path area. Get creative—and let's plant some seeds, sister.

GET IT TOGETHER

Pen and three pieces of paper
Basil seeds or a basil seedling
Pot filled with potting soil
Green paint or paint marker
3 shiny dimes or pennies

136   THE JOY OF HEX

Money & Success Attraction Oil *(page 132)*
or comparable oil
1 green chime candle
Chalice of water

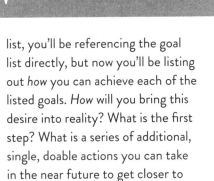

WITCH TIP: TRY A TUESDAY

Tuesdays are ruled by Mars, the god of action, so any goal-related spell (like this one) is extra effective when performed on this day of the week. Of course, you can do virtually any spell at any time and still get kick-ass results—but to give your goal-setting spell a little extra cosmic boost, try it out!

1 You'll begin this ritual by writing down a bullet-point list of your current career goals. Clear your mind and try to enter a meditative state where you're focused on what you *want* to achieve in your career. Think as big as you want—don't limit yourself! Once you've written it all out, try to boil down these lofty goals into a few concise intentions and goals. This is your goal list.

2 Once you're satisfied with that list, your next task is to grab another piece of paper, and make a second list (I know, there's a lot of writing for this one, so I hope your hand isn't too tired from scrolling on your phone all day!). On this list, you'll be referencing the goal list directly, but now you'll be listing out *how* you can achieve each of the listed goals. *How* will you bring this desire into reality? What is the first step? What is a series of additional, single, doable actions you can take in the near future to get closer to making this goal your reality? Write down your steps for each of the goals on your list.

3 Now it's time for one last list: your mantras. This list will once again reference your list of goals, but this time, you'll be rewriting them as "I" statements. For example, if your goal says, "I want to be promoted to manager of the XYZ department," or "I want to successfully launch my business," then write "I *am* the manager of the XYZ department," or "I *have* successfully started my business." This helps you take ownership of your goals—even though you haven't achieved them yet. Write a single "I" sentence to correspond with each of your goals.

4 OK, ready for a little plant magic? You'll be planting basil, which is not only a yummy herb that you can use in both cooking *and* witchcraft, but also a powerful tool for attracting money, career opportunities, and financial growth. Begin by using your green paint or paint marker to draw a money power symbol on your pot. You can use a pentacle or even a dollar sign if you'd like to keep it simple, or you can use a sigil that's designed to help you in achieving your goals, like this one:

5 Once the symbol has been drawn, fill your pot with soil, making sure to follow the directions for the basil seeds or seedlings you're planting. Then carefully plant the basil. Relate this process to your goals in your mind: Your goals are really just little seeds and seedlings right now, and they need attention, love, care, and tending if they want a good chance to grow. Once your seed is planted, shove three shiny dimes or pennies into the soil surrounding the seed for added luck and abundance.

WITCH TIP: BASIL BOOST

You can also harness the abundance-boosting power of basil by boiling the herb in water (fresh or dried) and then using the herbal infusion to wash your floors with. As you use the basil floor wash in your home, visualize your career goals coming into reality. Keep this in mind next time you have to mop your floor!

---

6 If you are using your money-drawing oil (or another comparable oil), use a few drops to anoint your green chime candle, coating the candle's surface by rubbing it from the base upward. Now put three drops of oil into the soil of the plant.

7 Place the anointed green candle next to the pot and light it. Green is a color often associated with luck, money, and abundance (as well as health and connection to nature!), which is why it's used in this ritual. Take your list of "I" statements and read them aloud as you pour some water from your chalice into the pot. Read this list aloud three times, and visualize each statement being true as you speak the words. Once finished, fold up that piece of paper three times and place it beneath the pot of basil or tape it onto the back.

8 As your green chime candle burns next to the basil, say the following spell aloud:

WITH THIS SEED I
PLANT MY DREAMS.
✦ *HYDRATED, NOURISHED,* ✦
. *BATHED IN SUNBEAMS,* .
WITH LOVE AND CARE,
THIS SEED I SOW.
I PLANT MY DREAMS AND
WATCH THEM GROW.

9 As a final step to your spell, review your list of action steps— what other steps should be added to this list? *Why* do you want to achieve these goals? Make yourself an actual, tangible to-do list and start working

on it. Display both your list of goals and action steps in a place in your home where you can revisit them daily. Allow your green chime candle to burn all the way down safely. Just as you'll follow your own direction for achieving your goals, also follow directions for how to properly care for your basil plant. Repeat your spell and/or reread your "I" statements each time you water the plant. Once the plant is grown, you should see progress and growth in your personal goals as well. If you'd like, you can transplant the plant into a larger pot or an outdoor garden (which can symbolically give your dreams more room to grow). Remember: You can harvest the basil leaves to use in recipes for some magickal kitchen witchery, or dry the leaves to use in other abundance spells.

PURSE FULL OF GOLD SPELL

○ ☽ ☽ ☽ ☽ ☽ ● ● ☾ ☾ ☾ ☾ ○

IS YOUR PURSE OR HANDBAG A HOT MESS? Don't lie, girl. If I were to dump it out right now in front of me, would I find a pile of bobby pins, crumbs, gum wrappers, and other mysterious paper shreds littering the essentials? Time to clean up that crap with a cleansing ritual that will both get your purse in tip-top shape *and* refine your mindset when it comes to making space for abundance. Here's a simple ritual to rid yourself of a scarcity mentality and maintain a positive attitude around money and the universe's ability to provide for you.

GET IT TOGETHER

All the purses/handbags in your current rotation

1 white chime candle

**Bundle of sustainably harvested sage
or other smoke-cleansing herbs**

1 small piece of pyrite crystal *(a.k.a. "fool's gold")*

Needle and thread *(or safety pin, if not sewing)*

Small piece of cloth, sized to wrap your crystal

Safety pin

---

1 The first step of this ritual is productive in more ways than one—but here, you have a chance to make an otherwise mundane task (cleaning out your purse or handbag) a magical one. Begin by opening your ritual space and lighting your white candle, which represents purity and clearing your path (cause that's what you're doing here, witches— clearing your financial path for more abundance!).

2 Grab all the purses that you're currently rotating through (maybe it's one, or maybe you're a lil' fashion witch and it's ten—whatever). Clear off a table top and dump the contents out entirely. If there's trash, old Chapsticks, crumbs, a random glitter eyeliner you've been searching for for *months*—clean it up! This is also a good time to wipe out the inside and clean off the outside of your purses with some moistened wipes. As you do your cleaning and organizing, imagine all the heavy financial stresses, toxic belief patterns, and bad money habits being wiped and cleansed and thrown away, too. This should feel like a fresh start, and not just a chore.

3 Now that you've cleaned these babies out and rid them of their actual gunk, it's time to cleanse them of their energetic gunk, too! Light your sage stick and allow the smoke to fill the inside of each purse, and cleanse the outside, too. Congrats, b*tch—your purses are cleansed!

4 Okay, now it's time to add a little positivity and luck to your money outlook by infusing your pyrite crystal with a spell. Pyrite is a stone of *major* abundance. It's glittery and eye-catching (just like gold!), and is super helpful for manifesting your goals into reality. The reflective energy of the pyrite will help to illuminate your spell and give it an extra sparkly power. Hold the crystal in your hand, and say the following spell aloud three times:

> **I AM ABUNDANT.**
> **MONEY FLOWS TO ME.**
> **I AM ABUNDANT,**
> **FREE AND EASILY.**

5 You've officially charged your pyrite crystal with your intention, making it all the more powerful! This is your lil' secret weapon. Next, turn your favorite purse inside-out, then take your needle, thread, and fabric, and sew the piece of pyrite into the lining of your purse, like a tiny pouch. If you're not such a crafty witch, simply wrap your crystal in fabric like a tiny sack, and then safety-pin it securely to the inner lining of your purse. Now your intention-charged pyrite is alchemized with your purse itself—and will be carried with you wherever you go, bringing you good luck and positivity when it comes to money.

LUCKY STAR FORTUNE JAR

○))))) ● ● (((((◯○

EVER HEARD OF A GOOD LUCK CHARM? This is one, but it's specifically tailored to bring you money and abundance! Perhaps the alchemy of these items plus your intention creates the magic. Or perhaps carrying this baby around will simply serve as a constant reminder that you, girl, are a lucky star—and a rich one, at that!

Do you have a piggy bank or a money jar in your room? Well, this fortune jar is here to replace that and give it a whole new and magickal twist. It serves a dual purpose, which is to 1) collect all your spare change, and 2) help to supercharge that change as a talisman in your spell and manifest it into more money. It's like your mystical savings account. Set this jar and candle somewhere in your room where you can see it and use it regularly.

GET IT TOGETHER

Large glass jar

Dried mint *(1 tbsp. or a generous sprinkle)*

Dried basil *(1 tbsp. or a generous sprinkle)*

Dried sage *(1 tbsp. or a generous sprinkle)*

Dried chamomile *(1 tbsp. or a generous sprinkle)*

Dried bay leaves *(as many as you'd like)*

Some spare change

Cinnamon

Gold glitter

---

1 In a large glass jar, mix together a blend of dried mint, basil, sage, and/or chamomile (feel free to adjust the suggested amounts based on what you have). On your bay leaves, write words that you associate with abundance, or any particular items that you're saving up for. To keep things general, you can skip this step and just throw in a few bay leaves without any writing on them.

2 Next, you're going to add in some spare change. Check your pockets and the bottom of your purse for loose coins. Add them one by one into the jar of herbs, holding each coin in your hand as you speak the following spell aloud:

AS SIMPLE COINS WILL FILL THIS JAR, I'LL ATTRACT MONEY FROM NEAR AND FAR. ABUNDANCE COMES SO EASILY BECAUSE I AM A LUCKY STAR.

3 Repeat this spell each time you throw a coin or a bill into the jar. Now sprinkle cinnamon over the contents of the jar and shake it up, mixing the coins together with the herbs. As a final step, sprinkle in a generous amount of gold glitter, which represents the illustrious element of gold, and the basis of most systems of wealth.

4 Anytime you feel your spell needs a boost, sprinkle a little bit more cinnamon inside the jar, add a bay leaf with an intention on it, or say the spell aloud as you offer up some more coins.

5 When your jar is full, empty it of its contents and sift out the coins for use. Dispose of the herbs by burying them or burning them in a firesafe bowl, or throwing them into a fire.

GODDESS OF LUXURY ABUNDANCE BATH RITUAL

○))))) ● ● ((((○

VENUS, APHRODITE, WHATEVER YOU WANT TO CALL HER— she's the goddess of love, beauty, pleasure, money, value, and luxury, baby. And when *we* want to feel rich and luxurious, all we have to do is channel her goddess-y nature through a ritual. This beautiful Goddess of Luxury bath ritual is ideal if you're ready to invite some serious abundance and luxuriousness into your life (and want to make a self-care night a whole lot more magickal while you're at it).

Ritual baths are a wonderful way to absorb the power of herbs, crystals, and candle magick and simply sit quietly with our thoughts to get in touch with ourselves. But they're also a prime opportunity to set a personal intention and cast a little spell—and if you're channeling Venus, this is a great time to work with one of your desires that feels *indulgent*. Part of this spell's practice is to allow yourself to want the sweeter and finer things in life. Don't limit yourself in your visualizations of abundance. Picture what you really want—see it, smell it, taste it, feel it, and mentally experience it on every level.

Sometimes, it can feel selfish to want luxury things for ourselves when there are so many people who have less than we do. But part of this ritual is embracing the fact that we—along with *every other person on the planet*—deserve abundance. And that part of asking for abundance is also asking for the ability to share abundance with others. Hoarding wealth is actually the opposite of abundance—that's greed. When we're willing to share, we should feel deserving of the good things that come our way. When you receive good things, celebrate them! Welcome them! Expect them!

That said, it's time to get in touch with your most indulgent, luxurious desires, and get comfortable manifesting them into existence. You deserve the finest things life has to offer, you lil' goddess, and it's time for you to start believing it.

GET IT TOGETHER

Coconut oil

Frankincense, patchouli, myrrh, bergamot, rose, sandalwood, and/or jasmine essential oils

Pink Himalayan sea salt

Roses

Citrine crystal

Seashell (optional)

Additional candles, crystals, mood music, or anything else to set the mood (optional)

---

1 Before you actually draw your bath, set a personal intention around money (and don't wait until the water's already running to come up with it, otherwise you might be stepping into a tub full of cold water!). Meditate on all the Venusian themes of luxury and value: What do you desire? What feels luxurious and valuable to you? What issues do you need to work through when it comes to how you value or how you experience pleasure? What makes you feel abundant? What sort of luxurious, pleasurable experiences do you want to have in your life? Let these questions guide you in some simple, personal intentions. Write them down, if helpful, so you can reflect on them as you soak.

2 Once your intentions are locked and loaded, prep your oil blend. Heat up ¼ cup coconut oil until it melts into a liquid. Then add a few drops each of frankincense, patchouli, myrrh, bergamot, rose, sandalwood, and/or jasmine essential oils (whatever you have is fine!), as these are all powerful luxury-enhancing, sensual, money-drawing oils. Mix them in with the coconut oil.

3 Draw your bath, and if you'd like to light some candles or put on some soothing music, go for it (ambiance is always good, especially when you're working with luxurious goddess Venus—she loves it!). Once you start filling the bath, allow yourself to connect with the element of water. Free-flowing, emotional, life-giving, and cleansing; embrace the qualities of water, and allow the fluidity of the element to loosen your energy.

4 Now think of your intentions, keeping that loose, watery mindset, and focus on it as you pour your oil blend into the bath water. Imagine the energy of the essential plant oils infusing your bath with possibilities and power. (Bonus: The coconut oil will also leave your skin feel highly moisturized and soft post-bath, which only adds to the luxurious energy you're manifesting.) Sprinkle in a small handful of the pink Himalayan sea salt. This is purifying and detoxifying, and will help to cleanse your spirit as you bathe. Finally, gently place an abundance of rose petals over the surface of the bath. Roses are the quintessential symbol of love, fertility, and attraction, and will help you stay present in your senses and attract whatever new luxuries you desire.

5 Enter your bath, bringing your seashell and citrine crystal with you (it's totally fine for your citrine to get wet, by the way). Seashells are symbolic of the goddess Venus, as according to myth, she was born of the sea (see Botticelli's famous *Birth of Venus* painting), which is why you're working with a seashell as a symbolic object. Hold the seashell in your hand to symbolize a connection to the goddess. In your own words, ask for permission to channel Venus's energy to help open yourself up to your intention.

6 Now hold the citrine crystal in your hands. Citrine is a bright, sunny, and powerfully positive crystal ally to help you feel confident that you deserve pleasure, abundance, and your own ability to manifest. Hold the citrine to your heart and close your eyes, envisioning the golden-colored energy field of the crystal opening up your heart to new possibilities, and allowing yourself to feel capable, optimistic, and worthy of your goals (revisit your list of intentions here!).

7 When you're ready, hold the citrine to your heart and say the following chant aloud:

> **I DESERVE LOVE.**
> **I DESERVE BEAUTY.**
> **I AM DESERVING OF LUXURY.**
> **I DESERVE PLEASURE.**
> **I DESERVE VALUE.**
> **I AM DESERVING OF ALL GOOD THINGS.**
>
> **I RECEIVE LOVE.**
> **I RECEIVE BEAUTY.**
> **I OPEN MYSELF TO LUXURY.**
> **I RECEIVE PLEASURE.**
> **I RECEIVE VALUE.**
> **I OPEN MYSELF TO ALL GOOD THINGS.**
>
> **I AM LOVE.**
> **I AM BEAUTY.**
> **I AM LIVING IN LUXURY.**
> **I AM VALUABLE.**
> **I AM ABUNDANT.**
> **I AM DESERVING OF ALL GOOD THINGS.**

8 Allow yourself to relax now. Connect with the vibrational energy of the citrine and with the goddess Venus's energy. When you're ready, you may step out of the bath. If possible, allow yourself to drip dry. Watch as the water drains, and envision your doubts, fears, and roadblocks around money and abundance slowly leaving your space, spiraling quicker and quicker out of your consciousness as the water drains from the tub. If you'd like, set the seashell on your altar as a token of Venus's luxurious presence and a symbol of the intentions set through your spell tonight. The spell is done.

WITCH TIP: LUXE AND LOVE

Venus is also the goddess of love, so if you'd like this bath to be more focused on your love life intentions, simply swap out the citrine crystal with a rose quartz, and use floral, sensual oils like ylang ylang and geranium in addition to rose and jasmine.

CHAPTER 8

WELLNESS SPELLS & RITUALS

HOW TO FOCUS ON YOU & MAKE SELF-CARE AN ACT OF MAGICK

Taking care of your soul's inner landscape and prioritizing your own goals, wellness, and self-care is vital if you want to be the most powerful witch (and the most high-vibe b*tch) that you can be. The right spells and rituals can help you go deep with yourself and put your health, productivity, and confidence at the forefront—right where it should be.

AS WITCHES, WE'RE CONSTANTLY DOING THE INNER

work and sorting through our sh*t to get to the root of our feelings, desires, and power. This is necessary work if we want to be the most powerful spiritual beings we can be (which, *duh*, we do!). Staying grounded, energetically clear, and in touch with our intuition is a huge part of being able to wield our power and energy effectively and cast spells that really *work*. But, news flash: we can't do that if we're not actively trying to take care of ourselves and prioritizing our wellness. That's just facts.

Not only are our spells less powerful when we're neglecting our own well-being— we also have less of a light to share with the rest of the world, and the people who can benefit from our power, too. Part of being a badass, healthy, and high-vibe person is contributing something to this world—speaking up for what's right, being there for other people, and using your little light for *good*. We don't live in a period of history where we have the luxury of being silent on issues that matter, so if you fancy yourself a witch and a lightworker, put your magick where your mouth is and make sh*t happen. Practicing self-care and honoring your personal needs is a win/win.

Reminder: Self-care is not selfish, y'all. It's really *necessary*, especially if we're trying to use our personal energy to create change in our lives (and hopefully the world around us, too). Spreading light 'n love 'n all that good stuff takes work—but if we're burnt out, anxious, overwhelmed, and overtired, then it's hard to find the energy to effectively contribute those powerful parts of ourselves to others, not to mention it'll be near impossible to feel happy or motivated to conquer our personal goals. **If we think of honoring our own needs and prioritizing wellness as part of our mystical practice rather than something adjacent to it, it might inspire us to make a little more time in our busy schedules for self-care.**

So yes, in order to make magick and attain "high-vibrational babe" status, we have to make time to care for ourselves. This includes our bodies, minds, spirits, and hearts (no skimping!). If we're constantly pouring everything out of our energetic cups, giving all we have to other people, things, and outside responsibilities (while ignoring our own needs, goals, and intuitions) then what's leftover when we need a little bit of that same TLC? You've gotta take care of *you*. If you know yourself and how to pamper that b*tch, then you can *always* come home to yourself at the end of the day. And no one can take that from you.

SELF-CARE IS MAGICKAL

We're busy b*tches, so we won't always have a ton of extra time to set aside for elaborate self-care rituals and luxurious goddess baths. That's why it's helpful to infuse a little more magick into your life in all sorts of other small-but-powerful ways:

- Put a few drops of a lucky money oil or mystical love oil into your body lotions and bath products to make your getting-ready-for-the-day routine more powerful.

- Keep some empowering crystals on your desk at work, and charge them with your personal intentions.

- If you spot a dandelion flower, set an intention as you blow off the seeds, which represent your wish spreading off into the universe to grow.

- Draw sigils on your notebooks, debit cards, or even on the bottom of your shoes to bring luck and magick with you wherever you go and into whatever you do.

TURN EVERYDAY ACTIONS INTO RITUALS

Since our self-care practices are already "rituals" of sorts (like cooking your fave comfort food or doing a ten-step skincare routine), almost anything you do can be treated like a spell—even the most mundane of tasks. Here are a few ways to do it.

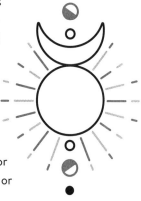

MAGICKAL MORNINGS

Come up with a positive mantra to start your day with empowerment and speak it aloud as you wash your face or brush your teeth each morning. You can also have a spell or mantra that you speak aloud in the shower.

NUMEROLOGY QUICKIE SPELL

If you see a lucky number on the clock (like 11:11, 2:22, 3:33, and so on), take this as a sign that you are on the right path, and say aloud, *"The universe is working in my favor, today and every day."* Do the same if you see the number anywhere—like on a building address or license plate, too.

ON-THE-GO PROTECTION

Do a quick mind-clearing meditation or protection spell on yourself while you drive, walk, or take the bus to work. Your commute, annoying as it might be, has potential to be a valuable break in the day to devote your mental energy to self-love and magick.

WITCH TIP: SOUND THE ALARM!

Give yourself an inspiring-as-f*ck mantra to help you start your day with a spell! Set your phone's alarm with a label that prompts you to perform a mini-spell before you even step out of bed for the day. It could be something as simple as "list your top three priorities today" or "list three things you are grateful for today." Speak them aloud and then follow it up with an affirmative statement, like "I will accomplish these things today," or "abundance in my life is endless." Voila! You've cast a spell before you've even put both feet on the ground.

KITCHEN MAGICK

Kitchen magick is real, girl. Consciously infuse your food with healing herbs as you cook (almost all herbs have powerful energetic properties, so make yourself aware of them so you can connect with their energy on a more conscious level!). Think of your kitchen as an apothecary!

MAGICKAL CHORES

Even cleaning your house and doing your chores can become a beautiful spell to purify your home (see page 162).

GLAMOUR WITCH QUICKIE SPELL

Everything you do can be infused with magick, including your beauty routine. As you cleanse your hair in the shower or wash your makeup off in the evening, say a mantra like "I cleanse away all that doesn't serve me and get closer to my truest self." When applying lipstick, say "I bring brightness and color to the world around me."

But obviously you're not limited to simply turning your daily maintenance routines into self-care spells. The full blown witchy spells and rituals that follow offer a deeper experience of witchcraft and more ways to invite self-care into your life.

WITCH TIP: A CASE FOR MONDAYS

Monday is believed to be ruled by the Moon, which is the planet that governs our emotions and most personal, inner world. You can do spells at any time, but spells focused on self-care can be especially effective on Mondays. Plus, a self-care spell is always a nice way to start the week!

INFINITE LOVE SELF-CONFIDENCE SPELL

AS WE MOVE THROUGH LIFE AND LEARN MORE ABOUT MAGICK, it's important to remember that we cannot control anything about other people. They can come and go from our lives as they wish, and they are free to feel however they feel. But there is one person you can always rely on, one person who can always be trusted—yourself. No matter what, no matter how shaky things could get, you will always be there for you.

That kind of ride-or-die energy and devotion certainly earns you the compassion, love, celebration, and appreciation that you'd show to your dearest friend or family member. Take a little time to foster the love, friendship, and appreciation you feel toward yourself with this infinity self-love spell. It's a great reminder that you're a cosmic being on a bizarre journey here on earth—so be nice to yourself.

GET IT TOGETHER

1 yellow chime candle

Large mirror *(can be fixed to a wall)*

Paper and pen

Handheld mirror

---

1 Make yourself comfortable in front of a mirror in your home, whether it's a mirror hanging in your room, bathroom, or anywhere else that you can get cozy. Light

the yellow chime candle in front of the mirror (yellow represents confidence and self-expression). As you light the candle, speak the following spell aloud:

*I FEEL, I LOVE, I
WORK, I DREAM,
I LEARN, I CREATE, LIKE
A STAR, I BEAM.
I LOVE MYSELF FIRST,
BEFORE ANYONE ELSE
BECAUSE THE UNIVERSE
MADE ME UNIQUELY MYSELF.*

2 Now say the spell again, and make eye contact with yourself in the mirror between each line. Say the spell aloud a third and final time—say it slowly, and allow yourself to really feel and believe the words you're speaking as you say them.

3 Take a moment to sit with your reflection. Get comfortable. Look into your own eyes, at your own face. Let your face relax—don't act like you're in front of a camera. Try to be as natural as possible, and simply observe. Now, with your pen and paper, write a short letter to yourself, as if you were writing a sweet letter to a friend. Address it to your own name, and write the things you appreciate about yourself. This is a letter of gratitude and celebration. It doesn't need to be long; a page or less is fine.

4 Now, grab your handheld mirror. Hold it below your face and turn it toward the other larger mirror in front of you, so that the two mirror reflections are facing one another. Position the handheld mirror so that it's reflecting your face in the larger mirror. You should see that it reflects an infinite portal of your image—your face within a mirror depicting your face within another mirror depicting your face within another mirror and so on. Start with the first and largest reflection, and look into your own eyes. Say, "I love you" aloud. Now move through the infinite series of reflections until they're too small to see (there will likely only be a few). Each time, tell yourself "I love you" as you gaze into the eyes of your reflection. Imagine yourself sending love to all the infinite "you"s in every possible version of reality. Maybe those "yous" are just like you, but not you. Don't you think they deserve love, too?

5 Now position your handheld mirror behind the yellow flame, and allow the yellow flame's reflection to enter the realm of infinite reflections of you. By reflecting this candle, you're offering a little bit of elemental candle magick to every version of you throughout the infinite realm. Love and magick, infinitely. Your spell is complete.

GET SH*T DONE ENERGY SPELL

○ ☽ ☽ ☽ ☽ ☽ ● ● ◖ ◖ ◖ ◖ ◖ ○ ○

MONDAYS, AMIRITE? But also, Tuesdays…, and Wednesdays…, and Thursdays…, and, well, damn! Livin' life can be exhausting, and it's not always easy to get motivated when we've got to-do lists a mile long but attention spans shorter than our pinky finger (and even fewer hours of sleep). If you need a lil' mystic motivation to help you get sh*t done, start your day with a sunny lil' energy-boosting spell to push you into your most productive state. And know that this natural energy enhancing spell isn't just for the morning time—you can do it at any point in the day, as long as the sun is still shining.

GET IT TOGETHER

Small bowl of cinnamon

Small bowl of coffee grounds

1 clear quartz, citrine, or garnet crystal

1 sprig of vervain
(dried or fresh) (optional)

Your list of priorities for the day

1 If possible, conduct this ritual outdoors, under the sunshine, as you're going to be harnessing the spirited and life-giving energy of the sun for your spell. Go outside with your supplies. To start, you're going

WITCH TIP: SWIRL SOME MAGICK INTO YOUR MORNING ELIXIR

Cast a mini-spell to help make your day productive while drinking your morning coffee or tea! Swirl your spoon in your cup in a clockwise motion three times as you state your personal intention for the day aloud. Then, with your spoon, seal your intention by drawing the shape of a symbol of your choosing—like a pentagram, cross, or heart—over the top of your beverage. Finish your morning elixir knowing that it's been infused with the energy of your intention. Then go slay the day.

to create a protective energy circle around yourself using the coffee grounds and cinnamon. Starting in front of you, sprinkle coffee grounds onto the ground as you turn in a clockwise motion, encircling yourself in the powder. As you sprinkle the coffee grounds, say "Today, I ask for energy." Do the same with the cinnamon; as you sprinkle it, say "Today, I ask for passion."

2 Next, hold your crystal, as you're going to use it as an energy conductor in your sun drawing meditation. Clear quartz will always amplify any energy and intention. Citrine is an energizing and motivating stone that encourages us to take action. And garnet can help us feel more productive and inspired. Any of these are great options—use what you have! Hold the crystal in your hands and position it so that it catches the sun's light. Watch it reflect and refract the powerful rays of the sun, feeling the warmth that the crystal is absorbing from this life force. Now hold the crystal over your stomach, which is just between your solar plexus chakra (which is located near your diaphragm represents self-expression and confidence) and your sacral chakra (which is located near your belly button and represents creative, productive energy).

3 Close your eyes and feel your entire being soaking up the sun's rays. Imagine your body pulling in this energy through every available avenue—your skin, your chakras, your hands, your feet. Now visualize the crystal in your hands radiating with the absorbed energy from the sun. Feel it filling you with creative energy and inspiration. Feel it also giving you pure confidence in your ability to work through your tasks for the day. Say the following spell aloud:

THE POWERFUL SUN, FULL OF LIFE-GIVING LIGHT, INSPIRE ME NOW FROM MORNING 'TIL NIGHT. THE CREATIVE FORCE OF THE POWERFUL SUN, PLEASE ENERGIZE ME 'TIL THE DAY IS DONE.

4 With your crystal still in your hand, read through your to-do list, stating aloud that you will do each task. Once that's complete, you may do a smoke cleanse on yourself and your circle by lighting up a sprig of vervain, which is an herb that sparks inspiration and brings positivity. Your spell is complete! Keep your crystal with you as a talisman as you work throughout the day, as it's now fully charged up with both your intentions as well as the sun's powerful, vital energy force.

CHILL WITHOUT THE PILL ANTI-ANXIETY SPELL

LIFE IS F*CKING STRESSFUL, and we all get anxious about stuff sometimes. It's a normal part of having a brain (and a life). And while feeling a healthy amount of fear about things can sometimes be helpful, spiraling into anxiety definitely isn't. Anxiety can hold us back from doing the things we want to do, and can totally suck up our energy, sending us into a dark spiral of negative, fear-based thinking. It can make small things feel like a huge deal, and lead us to obsess over things that may not even happen. Energy is a valuable resource (as you now know), so it's no good to waste it on negativity.

This super-simple anxiety banishing spell will help you clear away the anxious thoughts around any situation so that you can see things more clearly, relax, and bring a little extra positivity into the picture—in other words, it'll help you slay the day with a little less worry.

GET IT TOGETHER

Chamomile tea *(1–2 bags)*
Spoon for stirring
Lavender oil or fresh lavender

---

1 Brew a pot of chamomile tea. Chamomile is a common herbal tea made from the dried buds of the chamomile flower (you may even have some in your cupboard already). Whether consumed as tea or burned, it is often used to help bring about a more restful, relaxed state. If you have some dried lavender, try adding that to the blend, as it can also help with healing, purifying, and relaxation. If you have some moon water, you may add that as well (either before or after boiling the water).

2 Pour your tea, then sit down and think of the situation that is making you anxious. What's bringing you fear, dread, worry, or panic? When we're in the throes of anxiety, it's easy to feel like we've actually *become* the anxiety, and that this feeling is *part* of us. But the truth is that it's not. Anxiety comes and goes—our situations exist outside of our anxiety. Sometimes anxiety arises and makes us feel a certain way, but it does not define us and it is not *ours*. It's simply there.

3 Think of those very same anxiety-inducing situations and fears, but try to separate yourself from them. Reframe your thoughts to shape these feelings as visitors to the temple of your mind. They are not bad or evil visitors, but at the same time, they're not making you feel good. So acknowledge that they're there, but don't claim them as your own: They don't live there. They are feelings, separate from the facts. Now speak directly to these anxious thoughts: *"I see that you're here. But now I ask you to leave, so I can see the facts clearly and face this situation on my own."* Stir your chamomile tea in a clockwise direction with your spoon until it's cool enough to drink, and slowly begin to sip it, feeling the warmth of the water and the soothing

---

✦

WITCH TIP: QUICK CHILL

Need to chill fast? Try meditating with a lithium quartz crystal, which can diffuse your anxiety and bring a deep sense of calm.

✦

---

power of the chamomile to wash over you and flush away fear.

4 When we are anxious, often what's happening is that we've become overly focused on and fearful of the potential for a negative outcome—when that outcome isn't necessarily even going to happen. Now it's time to replace those thoughts with useful ones. As you sip your healing chamomile tea, visualize an alternative outcome of the very same situation that's making you anxious. Imagine what it would be like if everything worked out, and there was nothing to worry about. Imagine yourself being strong and handling the situation, and being okay in the end—even if it was hard or didn't go as planned. Imagine yourself experiencing this relief, ease, and positivity.

5 Now grab your fresh lavender, or if using lavender oil, either hold the open bottle to your nose or put a few drops on a piece of tissue paper or a cotton ball. Take several deep breaths of the lavender or oil in through your nose, and out through your mouth, allowing the flower's scent to really permeate through your senses and get into your body through its aroma. Lavender is a calming flower that promotes love, relaxation, and healing, so feel how these properties affect your state of mind as you inhale.

After a few deep breaths, say the following spell aloud:

✦ **I AM SAFE.** ✦
I AM LOVED.
THE UNIVERSE WANTS
WHAT'S BEST FOR ME.

6 Repeat this mantra as many times as you need. You can say it once or one hundred times, but you should repeat it until you believe the words are true and feel a sense of calm come over your being. Continue drinking your tea slowly and intentionally, stirring in a clockwise motion, as you consciously separate your thoughts from yourself, acknowledging and sending away the anxious feelings. Finish your tea, and the spell is done—and your anxiety should begin to subside.

WITCH TIP: FIRE ENERGY

This ritual incorporates the elements of water (tea), earth (flowers), air (aromatherapy), and a little fire (to heat the tea water). But if you'd like to add a heavier dose of fire energy, empty a second sachet of chamomile tea or chamomile flowers into a fire safe bowl or cauldron, and set the herb ablaze. The scent of the burning chamomile is known to help promote restful and relaxed feelings, and the smoke can be used as a cleanser.

BABE IN THE MIRROR BEAUTY SPELL

MIRROR, MIRROR, ON THE WALL, who is the fiercest one of all? B*tch, it's you! Time to up your confidence with this sweet, self-love-encouraging spell that you can easily incorporate into your beauty routine (or *any* routine) anytime you need a little confidence boost.

GET IT TOGETHER

Glass jar

Water

Rose petals

Rose quartz

Small glass spray bottle

Cloth

Lipstick

Mirror

---

1 In the morning, add some fresh water to a glass jar along with some fresh rose petals and a piece of pure rose quartz placed directly in the water. Let the jar sit in the direct light of the sun all day, either outdoors or in a sunny window. You may cover the jar with clear plastic wrap if you'd prefer not to leave it outdoors uncovered. You can also follow the instructions in Chapter 5 that explain how to make sun elixirs—but for this one, you'll include rose petals and rose quartz.

2 Once the sun goes down in the evening, your rose-infused sun elixir will be prepared. Strain out the rose petals and remove the rose quartz, then pour some or all of the elixir into a spray bottle (you can find small inexpensive spray bottles online, at the dollar store, or you can clean and reuse another spray bottle used for perfume or beauty products). You are now ready to begin your spell.

3 Go to the mirror you use most often to get ready and spray it down with the sun water, as if you're using a glass cleaner. Wipe it down with the cloth. Now spritz yourself with the sun water, starting just above your head and spritzing your way down.

Now look upon your reflection and say the following spell aloud:

> **AS I LOOK IN THE MIRROR, ALL I CAN SEE IS A BEAUTIFUL FACE STARING BACK AT ME. MY INNER BEAUTY SHINES OUT WITH LOVE. AS BELOW, SO ABOVE.**

4 Now grab your lipstick—any color will do, just make sure it's one you'd like to wear immediately! Draw the following sigil on your mirror with lipstick—it represents beauty, both inner and outer. You can make it as small or large as you'd like.

5 Put the lipstick on your lips. By using one of your own beauty tools as a magickal tool, you're infusing your beauty and self-care routine with power and magick. The sigil on your mirror will serve as a constant reminder to see the beauty in yourself, and to pamper yourself in the ways you deserve. Repeat this spell and incorporate it into your get-ready routine anytime you need a beauty-related confidence boost.

WITCH TIP: BRANCH BEYOND BEAUTY

You don't have to stick to this beauty-focused sigil alone when it comes to writing on your mirror! Modify this spell by using any sigil you feel you need at a given time—even if it goes beyond the realm of beauty and into other things, like love, money, or friendships.

MESSY WITCH HOUSE-CLEANSING & PROTECTION SPELL

○))))) ● ● ● ((((◯

IDEALLY, OUR HOMES ARE OUR SANCTUARIES AND SAFE SPACES—it's where we put up the feet, let the hair down, put the sweatpants on, and take the bra off—so we should make sure the energy there is tip-top. Why? Because while we can't control the energy of the outside people and places we come into contact with throughout the day, we *can* control (at least to an extent) the energy of our homes—and that's why it's so important to keep it both literally *and* energetically clean 'n sparkly.

This house-cleansing spell can be done anytime, but since it involves literally cleaning your house (yes, witches, that's required here—don't skip it!), it's good to sync it up to your usual chores-time anyway and do them as a double whammy. Plus, turning your chores into part of a ritual and spell makes it a lot more fun. Don't you love turning something mundane into something magickal? It's my favorite life hack ever.

If you don't have a whole-ass home to yourself yet (me neither, y'all), that's okay! You can certainly use some of these tips inconspicuously throughout your shared home, or you can simply perform the spell in a single room. As always, modify this to your personal witchy b*tch needs.

GET IT TOGETHER

1 white chime or 7-day candle

Florida water *(optional)*

Bundle of sustainably harvested sage
or other smoke-cleansing herbs

1 large bowl or cauldron

4 small bowls or clear glass jars

Sea salt

Rice

*(approximately 2 cups, or about ½ cup
for each small bowl or jar)*

Dried lavender

Cumin *(approximately ½ tbsp. or less)*

4 cloves of garlic

1 black chime or 7-day candle

---

1 What's the first step of this ritual? You got it—Clean up your living space. Open up all the windows to draw in a fresh, purifying airflow that'll break up any stagnant energy. This also brings in the element of air for your spell.

2 Start with a quick pick-up, clearing away and organizing any items that are on the floor, piled on surfaces, or out of place. Repeat the mantra *"When all my things are in their place, my magick has room to fill the space."* Take out the trash, gather up laundry, clean up dishes, and toss any old food from the fridge. You'll undoubtedly feel so much better once this is done. Clean off window sills, dressers, countertops, and other surfaces with a mild cleaning spray, or just some water mixed with a little white vinegar on a cloth. If you have it,

also sprinkle a few drops of Florida water into your cleaning mix or onto the surface you're wiping, as it'll do the double duty of disinfecting *and* spiritually cleansing the space. Once things are put away and cleaned, finish the job by sweeping and/ or vacuuming the floors. As a final step, do a smoke cleansing of your

WITCH TIP: STRAIGHT FROM THE WITCHES' BROOMSTICK

Always sweep and vacuum out toward the doors of your room and/or home—this energetically "sweeps" any spiritual dirt and negative energies outside instead of trapping it inside.

room or entire home. Begin at the door, then move clockwise with your incense or herbs, making sure to spread the smoke along the room's perimeter and up into the corners. As you cleanse, repeat the mantra, "Now that all my things are in their place, my magick has room to fill the space."

3 Now it's time to create some spell jars/bowls for your home. If you're only using it in your own bedroom or a single room of your house, you only need one. If you'd like to offer protection and cleansing to your entire home, you'll want to make four (one for each of the four cardinal directions: north, east, south, west).

4 Begin by lighting a white candle, which represents purity and brings some fire-element energy to the spatial cleansing you just performed. As you light the candle, speak the following spell aloud:

NO MATTER WHAT COMES OR WHO VISITS HERE, THE ENERGY WILL REMAIN PURE AND CLEAR.

5 Now, in a large bowl, combine salt, rice, dried lavender, and cumin powder. No need to measure ingredients; simply use amounts that

WITCH TIP: PEPPER POWER

Some people don't like the smell of cumin, so since this spell asks you to leave jars or bowls that contain it open in your home, feel free to substitute cumin with black pepper. Black pepper is also highly protective against bad energy—and it's even easier to find in your kitchen or the spice aisle of any market.

are compatible with what you have and what feels right—although go light on the cumin, as it can have a much more pungent smell than the other ingredients! The salt helps with purification and the continual cleansing of your home's energy; the rice brings luck and abundance; the lavender promotes peace, calmness, and restfulness within your home; and the cumin protects against negative energy and also theft. As you add each ingredient to the mixture, focus on the intention of each and what it adds to your spell, and visualize your home being spiritually clear, lucky, peaceful, and protected. If you're doing the spell throughout your home, separate this mixture into four jars or small bowls. If only performing the spell for one room, you can just use one single jar or bowl, and mix in a smaller amount of ingredients. Then place a single wrapped clove of garlic into each of the jars, atop the other ingredients. Garlic is one of the plant world's ultimate shields of protection against evil, bad juju, and negativity.

6 Now whip out your phone's compass and find the north, east, south, and west corners of your home. Place a jar in each of them. (Again, if only using in a single room, put it in any spot that works for you.) As you set the jars down, say the following spell aloud:

I ASK FOR GOOD LUCK AND GOOD VIBES THROUGH THIS SPELL. BRING PEACE AND LIGHT TO THIS PLACE THAT I DWELL, PROTECT MY HOME FROM HARM ALL NIGHT AND DAY, KEEP ALL NEGATIVITY FAR, FAR AWAY.

7 Now light the black candle, which offers protection and seals the spell. It is complete. Enjoy the energetically so fresh and so clean vibes in your living space. Repeat the spell and replace the ingredients in each jar whenever you feel they need a sprucing up. (You could do this in alignment with the new moons; or if they still feel fresh, just do it with the change of each season to draw in some fresh energy and give your space a deep clean.)

SPELL

SWEET DREAM SLUMBER PILLOW SPELL

SLEEP IS A MYSTICAL TIME OF OUR DAY DURING WHICH WE TRAVEL INTO ANOTHER REALM—the realm of our subconscious. As we astrally travel, our bodies have a chance to rest, recharge, and reset, while our subconscious can get out and roam wild 'n free, offering us tons of insight into the inner workings of our soul. Both our subconscious exploration time *and* our physical restoration time are all-important. So doing a spell to ensure restful sleep and sweet dreams can be a mystical and oh-so-pleasant way to relax before getting some zzzs and setting off on your nightly adventure through the mental ether.

Sachets full of herbs and charms are often used in spells and witchcraft, but for this sleep spell, we'll make a sachet shaped like a cute lil' pillow that you can keep with you in your bed through your nights' rest. It even includes a little pocket in which to place your nightly intention, if you're doing dreamwork or releasing particular worries during sleep. The sachet-creation portion is best done in the evening before bed, but once it's done, the energy infused into the pillow will continue to work its magick on you every evening (and you can recharge it with a quick spell before sleep at any time).

GET IT TOGETHER

Soft or silky fabric, cut into two 6-inch
squares and one 1.5–2-inch square

Needle and thread

As many of the following dried herbs as you can find
(*at least a couple heaping tbsps. of each, depending
on how stuffed you'd like your pillow*):
*Dried lavender, Dried chamomile, Dried lemon balm,
Dried valerian root, Pink Himalayan sea salt crystals, Lavender oil*

Dried piece of ginger root
(you can make this yourself by setting a small piece of fresh ginger root in the sun for a few days)

Paper and pen

1 small lepidolite, celestite, dream quartz, or lithium quartz crystal

---

1 Lay out your fabric. This is what you'll use to make your pillow. You are free to make your pillow larger or smaller, but I prefer a smaller pillow that you can nestle underneath your sleeping pillow, so as to keep it close to you as you rest (and not have to use a massive amount of dried herbs to fill it!).

2 But before sewing the pillow together, you'll want to sew on your intention pocket. Take the small piece of fabric (which should be cut into a rectangle or square) and using a needle and thread, sew down three sides in the center of one of the larger squares of fabric, so that it forms a pocket. If you don't know how to sew, that's okay—use any tight, simple stitch you can manage. Then, sew the two larger squares together, atop each other, sealing them on three sides to form a pouch. The larger square with the pocket sewn on should be facing the outside. And remember, for all you witches who don't stitch:

The pillow doesn't have to be perfect! In fact, its imperfections will add to its charm. It simply needs to hold the dried herbs in place once sewed shut.

3 Now, in a bowl or cauldron, mix together your dried herbs and pink Himalayan sea salt crystals. All the aforementioned dried herbs are great for promoting relaxation, calmness, sleep, and peaceful dreams, so use as many as you can find (you

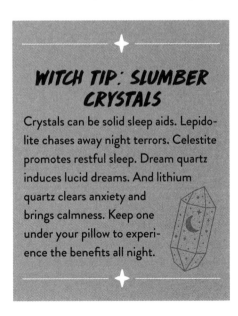

WITCH TIP: SLUMBER CRYSTALS

Crystals can be solid sleep aids. Lepidolite chases away night terrors. Celestite promotes restful sleep. Dream quartz induces lucid dreams. And lithium quartz clears anxiety and brings calmness. Keep one under your pillow to experience the benefits all night.

might discover some already in your tea or spice cabinet!). The pink salt is gently cleansing, which will keep your aura clear and your spirit protected as you snooze. Now sprinkle a few drops of lavender oil atop your herbs and salts, and mix it all up. This will make your blend smell even more potent and aromatic, as lavender is perhaps the most soothing, calming, anxiety-relieving, and sleep-inducing herb of the bunch.

4 Next, on a small piece of paper, write down the following spell:

✦ AS I LAY TO SLEEP AND ✦
CLOSE MY EYES,
I AM WATCHED BY THE MOON
IN THE STARRY SKIES.
MY BODY WILL REST AND
RECHARGE AND RESTORE
WHILE MY MIND IS FREE
TO FLY AND SOAR.
BRING ME A NIGHT
OF RESTFUL SLEEP
THAT IS DREAMY, PEACEFUL,
HEALING, AND DEEP.

5 Grab whatever crystal you'll be sewing inside your pillow and hold it in your hand. Speak the spell aloud three times—and as you do, envision the message programming into your crystal, making it even

more powerful in bringin' on a blissful night of zzzzs.

6 Now it's time to stuff that pillow! Open up the fabric pouch and gently scoop in your saltacious herbal blend until it's about three-quarters of the way full. Then fold up the piece of paper on which you wrote down the spell, and shove that baby right into the herbs. Do the same with the crystal that you programmed, too. Last but not least, stick in the piece of dried ginger root. Sleeping with ginger root is known to help keep bad dreams away, and no one needs bad dreams messing with their juju while they're trying to maximize on their beauty rest.

7 Top off your pillow stuffing with another scoop or two of herbs so it's nice and fluffy, then sew the fourth and final side of the pillow closed so the contents are nicely contained. Again, no need to morph yourself into a seamstress—it's okay if your pillow looks a lil' wonky and handmade—but do make sure it's sewn closed tightly enough that little piece of herbs and salt won't be sprinkling out between your sheets as you sleep.

8 Your spell is complete—but this cute lil' pillow is a mystical gift that keeps on giving! Keep the pillow in your bed with you to help you relax before you go to bed, get deep and restful sleep, and enjoy pleasant dreams. If you'd like to focus on a specific intention while you sleep, that's where the "dream pocket" comes in handy. Boil your night's intention down into a simple sentence or two, and write it on a small piece of paper. Then fold it up, stick it in the pocket, and place the pillow underneath or next to your regular pillow.

And remember, if there's a night where you need some extra sleepytime calm to help you wind down, simply hold the pillow in your hands and say the initial spell again aloud to reconnect with its magick—then hold the pillow to your face and take deep breaths so you can enjoy the yummy and soothing scents of the lavender oil and herbs. Sweet dreams, cuties.

WITCH TIP: SLUMBER SPARKLES

If you'd like to glitz out your mystical sleep sachet, feel free to get creative. Draw a calming, sleep-inducing sigil onto the fabric with puff paint for added power, or adorn the outside with fabric marker doodles, rhinestones, or anything else that'll make it extra glam and personal.

CHAPTER 9

SPELLS & RITUALS FOR YOUR SOCIAL LIFE

DEALING WITH LIFE & OTHER PEOPLE LIKE THE MAGICKAL B*TCH YOU ARE

Living life among other human beings can be one of the most enriching parts of our witchy lives, but it can also spark drama. That's okay! Conflict is often a chance to grow, and these spells and rituals can help keep your social circles running smoothly.

CHAPTER 8 WAS ALL ABOUT SPELLS THAT PRIORITIZE
YOUR INNER LIFE—your goals, your wellness, your confidence, your
energy level, and your overall self-care game. Très important and definitely a
foundational part of being the most powerful witch on the block. But now it's
time to flip this baby in reverse and consider the parts of your life that are more
externally focused, like your friendships, your social life, and the interactions
you have with other people and energies all day long (both in person and
virtually). Even if you're a solitary witch, you're still influenced by friends, family
members, roommates, and everyone you follow on social media (yes, scrolling
through your feed counts as interacting with outside energy, too!). Our
relationship to outside energy can (and should) be enriching, and the people and
social situations we find ourselves with should be fun, inspiring, and energizing.

However, not all of our encounters with other people are intentional—and when
they are, it doesn't necessarily mean they'll be without issues or struggles! Like
all things, it works both ways; sometimes our relationships and interactions
with other people (friends and family included) can be draining, dramatic, or
stressful. *Le sigh.* Jealousy happens. Arguments happen. Trolling happens.
Hurt feelings happen. Unwanted attention happens. And
sometimes loneliness happens, too, due to a lack of energizing
relationships in your life. Performing a spell or ritual to help
you support yourself in dealing with these situations as they
come up is a super-empowering way to take charge and
start protecting your energy from the influence of others and
resolving negative feelings that can arise from social interactions.

You might notice that some of these spells could also come in handy
in your love life—for things like stopping drama, sweetening up a situation, or
banishing jealousy—which are all applicable to the issues that can often spring
up in romantic relationships. But it's important to remember that we form
relationships of all kinds with everyone we encounter. Obviously, we have
unique romantic relationships with our lovers, but we also have different but
equally close (and sometimes equally complicated) relationships with friends
and family members, too. That means that there are plenty of spells that can be
modified and used in all sorts of situations. Feel free to adapt any of these spells
to fit a situation in your love life, too!

EVERYDAY MAGICK FOR THE SOCIAL WITCH

- **Get dressed with glamour magick.** Getting dressed to go out and meet with friends? Bring color magick into your makeup and wardrobe! Wear red if you're feeling passionate, or if you need to stay grounded and rooted. Wear orange during times when you're trying to make new friends, be creative, or feel social. Wear yellow if you're feeling low and need to boost your confidence or add some extra positivity to a situation. Wear blue to help with communication; it'll help you find your voice and handle potentially awkward convos with your boss. Wear green or pink if you're feeling flirty, or if you need to bring some compassion into a situation. And finally, wear indigo and purple if you're looking to feel more spiritual, personally empowered, and trusting of your own intuition.

- **Don't forget your stoner friends.** I'm talking about *crystals*, guys, c'mon now. Crystals are helpful for just about anything, but some can be major do-gooders when it comes to your social life—and literally all you have to do is throw one in your purse or pocket and you're good to go. Blue lace agate can help you find all the right words and sail through tough conversations. Carnelian is a huge confidence-booster that'll help you overcome shyness. Yellow jasper helps you to be less sensitive and more fun-loving. And chrysoprase can strengthen your friendships and make you more open to deep connections with people in your life.

- **Collect your coven.** If you have other friends who are interested in witchcraft or are into spirituality, why not plan a spell together? Almost all the rituals and spells in this book can be modified to be worked with a group. The most important thing is that you communicate with your friends first and ensure you all feel comfortable. Having multiple people performing a spell together simultaneously can actually bring a *ton* of powerful energy into it—and can totally bond you with your friend(s) on an entirely new level, too! However, if you feel overly shy or self-conscious about performing any part of the spell or sharing your intentions with someone else, then you might be better off conducting the spell solo—and that's okay too!

- **Throw a party for a witchy holiday.** If you don't have friends who want to do spells with you (or if you simply prefer to perform your magick solo) but still want to bring a social element into your practice, consider hosting a gathering for one of the sabbats, which are witchy holidays that take place throughout the year. Most of these holidays coincide with other notable dates (such as Halloween, May Day, and the start of each new season), so it can be a novel way to celebrate a traditional witchy festival in a way that's entertaining for everyone, whether they're into witchcraft or not. Try throwing a fun bonfire complete with a DIY flower-crown-making booth for the Summer Solstice, or a host a cozy holiday gathering with mulled wine and candles for the Winter Solstice.

- **Turn Jewelry into a Magickal On-the-Go Amulet.** A piece of jewelry can turn into a protective amulet or lucky charm if you properly charge it up with your intention. Incorporate the charm into one of your spells, then hold it in your hand as you say the spell aloud. After saying the spell (but before closing the ritual), say aloud, "And may this [item] bring me [intention] any time it's by my side. So it is."

SWEET AS SUGAR LUCK SPELL

○ ☽ ☽ ☽ ☽ ☽ ● ☾ ☾ ☾ ☾ ○

IF THERE'S A SITUATION THAT YOU'D LIKE TO ENSURE GOES YOUR WAY AND REALLY DON'T WANT TO TAKE A CHANCE ON, try this sweet as sugar luck spell, which will quite literally *sweeten* up any situation you're facing and bring you loads of luck. It's extraordinarily uncomplicated, but it's so powerful—this is why "sweetening" spells that involve putting something in a jar of sugar (or another sweetener) are so dang common. Easy and effective, this spell works especially well for things like tough conversations, negotiations, or any other sticky sitch in which you don't have a lot of control over outside factors, and want to bring some added luck and compassion into the equation.

This spell uses easy-to-find supplies that add a big ol' dose of positivity to any pursuit, which can make even something that's awkward and stressful a little easier to navigate and more palatable overall. A spoonful of sugar makes the medicine go down, remember? So amp up the lucky vibes and sweeten up any sitch using this quick and simple spell.

GET IT TOGETHER

Paper and pen
Glass jar with a metal lid
Sugar
1 chai tea bag
1 green aventurine crystal (optional)
Clovers (optional)
1 pink candle

SPELL

1 On a piece of paper, write down the details of the situation you need assistance with. You can make it long or short, but just be clear about the matter at hand. Remember, it's not advisable to make your spells about an individual person, so focus on the outside details and circumstances of a situation rather than the people involved in it. Once you've finished writing, fold up the paper.

2 Now pour enough sugar in the jar to cover the paper but do not fill it to the top (you may also use maple sugar, agave nectar, or another sweetener in place of the sugar). Empty a sachet of chai tea into the jar with the sugar (the herbs in chai—such as cardamom, ginger, cinnamon, clove and others—can all help in adding energy, sweetness, and luck to your spell). If you're using some clovers, place a few on top of the sugar, as these represent good luck and cheerfulness (yes, even if they don't have four leaves!).

3 Put your folded paper into the sugar in the jar. To make the spell even more powerful, place a green aventurine crystal in the jar, as this is considered one of the luckiest crystals around. Seal up the jar and, to ensure your paper is buried in the sugar blend, shake it up if you'd like.

4 Now grab a pink candle (pink brings joy, compassion, and positivity, which is ideal for this spell) and place it carefully and safely atop the sealed lid of the sugar jar (you can put it right next to the jar if it doesn't feel sturdy or if the candle or candle holder is too large). Light the candle, and then say the following spell aloud:

I CALL ON THE POWER OF SUGAR AND SPICE TO BRING ME GOOD LUCK AND MAKE EVERYTHING NICE. EASY AND BREEZY, LUCKY AND FREE, SWEETEN UP THIS [DEAL, TALK, DAY, INTERVIEW] FOR ME.

5 When your candle has been burning for long enough, pour some of the hot wax over the sealed lid of the jar, letting it dribble around the edge and sides of the jar, sealing it up even further with the consecrating power of the flame. Then allow the candle to continue burning next to the jar. Once the candle is out, place the jar on your altar or in a safe spot in your home. Return to the jar each day and hold it in your hand, shaking it gently as you repeat the words of the spell. Do this until the situation has resolved itself and passed—hopefully with plenty of luck and sweetness.

DRAMA-DROWNING FREEZER SPELL

LOVE IT OR HATE IT, drama *happens*. Occasional hurt feelings, badmouthing, and disagreements are basically an inevitable part of having a circle of friends, a family, or a relationship.

If there's gossip and drama going down within your squad, in your relationship, or at home with your roommates or family, then it's time to stop, drop, and *freeze*. Freezer spells are often used to stop something dead in its tracks. This simple version can help drown any drama that's currently mucking up your situation.

GET IT TOGETHER

Paper and pen
Clove oil (*optional*)
Glass jar or plastic food storage bag
Dried cloves

---

1 Write down everything that's going on in the situation that's dramatic or causing discord. Remember, this spell isn't about binding anyone or controlling anyone's actions—it's simply about diffusing drama. So try to leave out any references to individual people, and instead focus on the unnecessary drama surrounding a situation. If you have clove oil, place three drops of it onto the piece of paper (as clove is known to help banish gossip.

2 Now it's time to drown this drama once and for all. Fold up the piece of paper and place it inside the jar or bag. Fill the jar or bag with water (but don't fill it all the way up, as water expands when it freezes, so you'll need to leave some space). As you do, envision the drama "drowning" and totally losing access to all oxygen, as if you're extinguishing a flame. Seal the jar or bag, and place it inside your freezer. Say the following spell aloud:

FREEZE THIS DRAMA IN ITS TRACKS. NO RUNNING MOUTHS OR STABBING BACKS. DROWN THIS DRAMA, LET IT CEASE.

3 Leave the jar or bag in your freezer until the situation has resolved and the drama has been diffused. Feel free to use clove oil regularly during this period to help aid the gossip-stopping power of this spell, such as by diffusing it or putting a few drops in an oil burner. Once the situation *does* resolve, it's time to wrap up the spell's final step. Take the jar or bag out of the freezer and allow it to thaw so the water is liquid again. Go outside and find a patch of dirt where you can dig a small hole. Remove the paper on which you wrote about the drama, and place it in the hole. Now pour the water in on top of it. Finally, sprinkle some dried cloves in the hole (to help keep the drama at bay for the long term), then bury it all back under the dirt. The spell is done.

SOCIAL MEDIA MAGICK SPELL

○)))) ● ● (((((○

AT THIS POINT, SOCIAL MEDIA IS AN UNAVOIDABLE PART OF OUR LIVES. And that's not a bad thing. While it may ultimately amount to just a bunch of pixels on a screen, social media has the power to connect us with people, inspire us, and bring us closer together. On the flip side of the coin (cause ya know, there's *always* a flip side to the coin), social media can also get super toxic. It can certainly stir up some drama in our friendships, our romantic endeavors, and even ravage our self-esteem. And it can be addicting, and no one wants to be glued to their phone! We've got important sh*t to do and magick to make in the real world.

That's why every once in a while, it's a good idea to cleanse your social feed with a little bit of magick. This oh-so-simple social media spell can help you banish negativity from your feed, diffuse drama that's starting online, and infuse your social media presence with a lil' extra sweetness—all using the power of emojis.

GET IT TOGETHER

Your phone

Feather (*must be found, not purchased*)

1 white chime candle

---

1 Grab your cell phone and your feather (which represents the element of air), and use the feather like a tiny magick broom by sweeping it upwards, from the bottom of your phone to the top. Do this on both sides of your phone. The airy element of the feather brings a light and airy energy to the spell—a reminder that social media use should be something light and fun rather than heavy and intense. If you don't have a feather, simply use your hand and visualize a cleansing light sweeping away heaviness and negativity.

2 Once you've finished your lil' energetic "sweep," open up the social media app on your phone that you'll be working the spell on. Scroll back to the very first post in your feed. This post marks the beginning of your journey on the platform, so this is where you're going to do some symbol work. But instead of using a sigil, you're going to use the symbolic language of social media: the emoji. On the first post in your feed, leave a comment with nine consecutive emojis. You can use nine of any of the following emojis, depending on what your spell is focused on:

Evil eye ⊙ = To keep away the judgment and negativity of haters.

Salt shaker = To cleanse away any current drama.

Pot of honey = To make your feed feel more positive and supportive.

Four-leaf clover = To bring business or networking opportunities.

Butterfly = To help you gain popularity.

3 Once the comment is posted, it's time to get working on the IRL magic. Light your single white candle, and say the following spell aloud. You'll only say *one* of the five options—whichever spell corresponds to the emoji you chose to use.

[WITH THE EVIL EYE I SAY, KEEP THE HATERS AWAY.]
[WITH SALT I SAY, KEEP THE BAD VIBES AWAY.]
[WITH HONEY I SAY, BRING POSITIVITY MY WAY.]
[WITH THE CLOVER I SAY, BRING OPPORTUNITY MY WAY.]
[WITH THE BUTTERFLY I SAY, BRING A FOLLOWING MY WAY.]
LEVEL UP MY FEED, SERVE ME EXACTLY AS I NEED.

4 Now, to consecrate your symbolic candle lighting in the virtual realm, go back to that first post and leave another comment—this time just a single candle emoji, to represent the flame that you're burning here in the physical realm to set your spell into motion. And so it is.

"THINK PINK" JEALOUSY MELTING SPELL

○ ☽ ☽ ☽ ☽ ☽ ◗ ● ● ◖ ◖ ◖◖ ◖◖ ○

JEALOUSY IS THE WORST, BUT IT'S A FEELING THAT EVERYONE—even the most confident people among us—have to deal with at some point or other. This unpleasant emotional visitor is common in relationships, both romantic and friendly, but we can experience jealousy in all sorts of situations. We could feel envious of a celebrity, of someone we see on social media, or even of our own best friend. But jealousy is one of those emotions that just doesn't serve us. We should be focused on being our finest, baddest, bestest self rather than wasting our energy wishing we had something that someone else has.

Jealousy also sucks when you're on the receiving end of it. If someone is jealous of you, they might be thinking negatively about you, rooting against your success, or treating you with resentment because of their own insecurities. This spell can help to melt away any covetous negative energy being sent your way because of jealousy, and can protect you from the bad vibes that haters send.

Jealousy is nicknamed the "green monster" (and damn, it sure is a lil' monster), so we're going to counteract it by using color magick and embracing the color opposite to green on the color wheel: pink! So let's get all pretty in pink and do the damn thing.

GET IT TOGETHER

Green marker, pen, or colored pencil

Pink marker, pen, or colored pencil

Paper

Firesafe bowl or cauldron

Black pepper (*yep, the stuff from your kitchen!*)

---

1 On a piece of paper, use a green pen (green crayon, colored pencil, or marker works, too) to write down all your feelings around whatever it is you're feeling jealous about (or alternately, the feelings of envy you perceive from others). Let this be a cathartic brain dump for you. It's okay to get worked up, too! Let it *all* out on paper, even if you fill a full page with your green script. Purge it the f*ck out of you.

2 Next, you're going to use a sigil that is designed to protect you against jealousy (although feel free to use your own if you'd like to design one yourself). Using your pink pen or marker, draw this sigil, large and thick, right on top of your page of green text.

3 Let it overlap all the words, filling the whole page with the pink image of the sigil. This creates a pink, symbolic shield to start protecting you from these thoughts.

4 Let's burn these jealous, sh*tty thoughts, once and for all. In a firesafe bowl or your cute lil' cauldron, set fire to the piece of paper. Shake some black pepper over the flame as the paper is burning (black pepper is great for banishing all sorts of feelings of negativity, including jealousy). This helps to solidify the banishment.

5 As the paper burns, speak the following spell aloud three times:

> *JEALOUSY IS UNWELCOME HERE. I INVITE IN LOVE, AND I BANISH FEAR.*

6 Now it's time to melt the jealousy away using your own self-love and self-compassion—because that's exactly what jealousy often eats away. Get in a comfortable, quiet position and close your eyes. Mentally feel into your chest area, where your heart is. You're going to be opening up your heart chakra, which is the energy center of your body that gives and receives love, compassion, kindness, and gentleness—all of which you need right now, sister. Visualize a bright, glowing, bubblegum pink light begin to emanate out of your heart chakra and beam all around you, bathing you in light. Visualize the glowing pink light melting over you. Pay attention to what it feels like; perhaps it's warm and sweet, or cool and soothing—you decide. Continue to envision this light swirling around your body. In your mind, repeat the mantra from earlier as you visualize the pink light.

7 Wrap up the ritual when you feel fully connected to your heart chakra and bathed in the beautiful pink glow. Repeat this spell any time you're feeling the stab of someone's jealousy toward you, or whenever *you* feel jealous of someone else and want a reminder that you are enough just as you are.

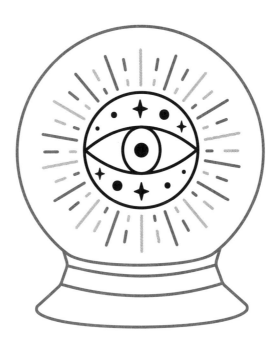

SPIRITUAL BUG SPRAY

○))))) ● ● ((((C○

BUGABOOS: They don't just come out in the summer anymore. Just like no one wants to be swarmed by mosquitos or have their space taken over by ants, it's also a major downer when a person or energy is cramping your style, violating your space, or bringing down your vibe. Whether it's a negative Nancy from work, a passive-aggressive roomie, or a random catcaller throwing all kinds of unwanted attention your way, it's time to whip out the bug spray to keep them buggies at bay—and I'm talkin' about a bug spray of the *spiritual* sort.

The following ritual involves creating your own herb- and crystal-infused potion to keep your aura and energy clear. It also involves a spell that you can use anytime you feel the need to get your spritz on and exterminate the bad vibes. Use it around your body to protect your personal energy field, or spray it around your home to clear any heavy or unwanted energies.

GET IT TOGETHER

Small glass spray bottle

Witch hazel

Small pieces of smoky quartz crystals
(as many as you'd like, although just a single crystal piece will do)

Sea salt

Rosemary *(herb or oil)*

Lavender or geranium *(herb or oil)*

Peppermint *(herb or oil)*

Citronella oil

Distilled water or moon water

If you are using fresh or dried herbs in your spray *(instead of oils)*, you'll need to infuse the witch hazel with the herbs first to make it potent.

WITCH TIP: WITCH HAZEL INFUSIONS

Make a spell-ready witch hazel infusion that extracts extra power from dried herbs. Put your dried herbs (up to 1 cup) in a mason jar and then fill the jar with witch hazel, covering the herbs by about an inch or so (as the herbs need room to expand). Place the jar in a cool, dark place for about two weeks, and shake up the jar every day. If the herbs expand beyond the surface of the witch hazel, top it off with a little bit more witch hazel to ensure they're covered (otherwise they could rot). After about two weeks, you'll see that the witch hazel is infused with the herbs and their color, smell, and healing benefits, too. Strain out the herbs. You're ready to begin your ritual and spell.

1 If you are using essential oils instead of herbs, skip the step above and start here. Fill a glass spray bottle about halfway with witch hazel (if you've infused your witch hazel with herbs, use that). Drop in one or multiple small smoky quartz crystals, which will infuse the water with a spiritually protective and deeply grounding energy to keep you centered and rooted. Then add a couple of pinches of sea salt, which has additional purifying and cleansing benefits. Add in whichever essential oils you'll be using (anywhere between 5 to 15 drops of each, depending on the size of your bottle, of course). Rosemary, citronella, and peppermint all have protective and negativity-repelling properties, while lavender and geranium are great for soothing the stress brought about by the energetic "bugs" you'll be telling to buzz off. Finally, top off the bottle with either plain distilled water or moon water. Seal it and then shake, shake, shake it up. Your spiritual bug spray is *done*.

2 Now it's time to use it. When you're ready to use your spray and work some pest-control magick on the negative energies funking up your space, say the following spell aloud as you spritz yourself and/or the space around you:

WITH THIS POTION
I CLEAR MY SPACE.
ALL UNWANTED ENERGY
MUST RETURN TO ITS PLACE.

YOU'RE UNWELCOME HERE—
BAD VIBES I'LL REPEL.
I AM BALANCED
AND SHIELDED
UPON SPEAKING THIS SPELL.

3 Now that your potion is created, you can use it anywhere and anytime you need to rid yourself of unwanted energy, attention, or situations. Repeating the spell out loud as you spritz will make it even more energetically potent, and will more deeply empower you to set boundaries and deflect unwelcome vibes. And remember, always shake up this baby before spraying—it not only mixes the oils with the water (which is necessary, since oil isn't water soluble), it also "shakes up" the power of the protective spray, activating its ingredients and charging the potion with the energy of your movement.

4 Now shoo those energy flies away and don't let 'em bother you.

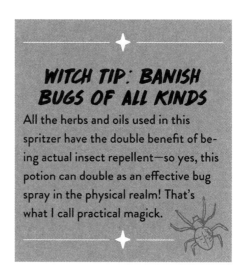

WITCH TIP: BANISH BUGS OF ALL KINDS

All the herbs and oils used in this spritzer have the double benefit of being actual insect repellent—so yes, this potion can double as an effective bug spray in the physical realm! That's what I call practical magick.

SPIRIT SQUAD FRIENDSHIP MANIFESTATION SPELL

YOU'RE A SOLID, CAPABLE, ONE-OF-A-KIND WITCH B*TCH ALL ON YOUR OWN—and hopefully, you know it! But obviously, it's nice to have like-minded friends around who are down to throw a few tarot spreads, get real, and stay up late talking about the mysteries of the universe—although, to be quite honest, it's not always easy to find 'em.

There are lots of reasons why you might want to open yourself up to new friendships. Maybe you just moved to a new city. Maybe you started at a new job or school. Or maybe you're just realizing that not all your friends *get* you, and you're looking to expand your circle. As you grow and evolve (and start getting more in touch with your higher, badass, spiritual self), you might find that it's harder to connect with people or find friends who really *get* your vibe. And can I let you in on a secret? That's *normal*. Not everyone grows in the same direction as the people around them and that's okay! In fact, it would be weird if you did. Doing this simple spell will help you put out the feelers for new friendships and bonds with people who are on your level.

GET IT TOGETHER

1 yellow altar candle

Carving tool

Clove oil

3 small tea light candles

4 shot glasses

Items symbolizing air and earth elements

A glass full of lemonade or lemon tea

---

1 Yellow is the color of friendship, which is why we're using a sunny, posi-vibes yellow altar candle to bring some warmth and energy to this spell. Use a carving tool (you don't need anything fancy—whatever works!) to inscribe the following sigil into your yellow candle. This symbol is designed to help attract like-minded people who will get your vibe and jive with your energy.

2 Anoint the candle using a drop or two of clove oil (you might want to mix with a little carrier oil like jojoba or coconut, as clove oil is particularly spicy and could be irritating if you have sensi skin). Rub the oil over the surface of the candle and the sigil starting from the bottom and pulling upward, toward the wick. Clove is helpful in banishing drama, gossip, and negativity, so it'll weed out any fair-weathered friends as you perform this spell, leaving space only for the positive ones.

3 Now that your candle is carved and anointed, let's set the stage for the ritual and spell. On your altar or on a table in front of you, set out the three small tea light candles in a triangle shape: one directly across from you, and then one to your left and right, closer to you. The three tea light candles plus you represent the completion of a quad. There are lots of iconic quads in witchcraft and nature—four elements, four seasons, four directions, you name it. While this spell may attract more or less than three new friends, having a total of four flames brings an energy of balance, fullness, and representation, which is what you're attracting in a new friendship.

4 Place a shot glass next to each tea light candle, then place the fourth shot glass in front of you. Either in the middle of the candles or just in front of you, set up your yellow candle. As mentioned, we're trying to bring the energy of balance and representation here. The candles represent fire energy and the cups represent water energy, so now get out whatever sacred item you'll be bringing in for air and earth energy (like incense or a feather for air, and a crystal or plant for earth) and add them to your spread.

5 Light the candles now, beginning with the anointed yellow candle and following it up with each of the tea lights, starting with the one on your left and moving clockwise from there, ending with your own. Now say the following spell aloud:

> *WHETHER OR NOT WE*
> *AGREE ALL THE TIME,*
> *I ASK FOR FRIENDS WHO*
> *CONNECT WITH MY MIND.*
> *SUPPORTIVE TOGETHER,*
> *SUPPORTIVE APART,*
> *I ASK FOR FRIENDS WHO*
> *CARE FOR MY HEART.*
> *IN TIMES OF STRUGGLE*
> *AND IN TIMES OF WEALTH,*
> *I ASK FOR FRIENDS WHO*
> *SUPPORT MY HEALTH.*
> *COMPANIONS WHO MAKE*
> *LIFE FEEL MORE WHOLE,*
> *I ASK FOR FRIENDS*
> *WHO SEE MY SOUL.*

6 Let's serve up this spirit lemonade, shall we? Pour a bit of lemonade into each of the four shot glasses (yours included). Lemons (in all forms) have long been used in friendship spells, as their bright and citrusy energy attracts positive and long-lasting friends into your life. You can use any lemonade you'd like— even if it's just lemon juice squeezed into water with sugar, DIY-style!

7 Hold up your shot glass and clink the glass to your left and say, "cheers to new friends who I can connect with intellectually." Now clink the glass across from you and say, "cheers to new friends who show me affection and support my goals." Clink the glass to your right and say, "cheers to new friends who are emotionally open and supportive." And finally, hold up your own glass and say, "cheers to friends who appreciate my soul." Drink your shot of lemonade, taking in the energy of positivity and new possibilities.

8 Allow the candles to burn down safely. You may drink the other three shots of lemonade, or pour them outside into the soil (but do not pour them down the drain—you want to recycle this mystical offering back into the earth instead of treating it like waste!). This spell will bring opportunities! Stay open to new friendships and connections.

WAY BACK IN THE INTRODUCTION of this book,
I told you about Witch Rule #1: You are f*cking powerful. After
taking this lil' crash course in spells and rituals (and hopefully getting
a few under your belt), I hope you believe it more than ever.

There will always, always be obstacles that stand in the way of us and our
dreams. Life isn't perfect, and nothing—no spells, no witchcraft—can change
that. But to know that you have something inside you that can't be taken away?
That's a game-changing realization. Through witchcraft, you start a new kind of
relationship with the unknown. You enter a conversation with the mysterious
elements of nature and the universe. You start working with the invisible forces
of energy and connecting with the power of nature. How incredible is that?

Perhaps even more importantly, though, witchcraft involves getting in touch
with the deepest parts of *yourself*. It's about learning to listen to yourself. Trust
your intuition. Honor your desires. Believe in your power. Communicate with
your subconscious. Heal. The mysterious energy of magick isn't just out there,
somewhere. It's in *you*, girl. Don't forget it.

One more thing to commit to memory is Witch Rule #2: Fuck the rules.
You do *you*. Follow your own heart. If you act with intention and stay in
touch with your higher self, you will always make the right choices.

So, my little witch baby, allow your days to fill up with magick.
Understand that all your actions can be rituals; understand that all your
words can be spells. If you set aside the time, energy, intention, and
reverence for magick, then it will arrive. Plain and simple.

Call it "magick" or simply call it yet-to-be-explained, spells and rituals *work*.
I hope you'll keep indulging in the absolute *joy* of hex.

And so it is!

INDEX